WOMEN'S INSTITUTE
SOUPS
for All Seasons

LIZ HERBERT

SIMON &
SCHUSTER

LONDON · NEW YORK · SYDNEY · TORONTO

Acknowledgements

I would like to thank all those from far and wide who have so kindly helped me. Including my willing band of tasters, and husband, Nigel, for keeping the world turning whilst I wrote this book!

First published in Great Britain by Simon & Schuster UK Ltd, 2008
A CBS Company
This paperback edition first published 2009

Simon & Schuster UK Ltd
1st Floor, 222 Gray's Inn Road, London WC1X 8HB

The right of Liz Herbert to be identified as the Author of this Work has been asserted by her in accordance with sections 77 and 78 of the Copyright, Designs and Patents Act, 1988.

1 3 5 7 9 10 8 6 4 2

Design: Fiona Andreanelli
Food photography: Ian Garlick
Home economist: Lorna Brash
Stylist: Liz Belton

Stock images:
page 11 © 2005 iStock International Inc. All rights reserved.
page 19 © Ariusz | Dreamstime.com
page 51 © Chrisharvey | Dreamstime.com
page 81 © Izanoza | Dreamstime.com
page 111 © 2005 iStock International Inc. All rights reserved.

Printed and bound in China

ISBN 978-1-84737-179-9

Contents

Introduction

Clear and soothing, piquant and satisfying, chunky and warming, how do you like yours?

Soups come in all manner of tastes, colours, textures and consistencies. When I was first asked to write this book I imagined that it would all be quite straightforward – after all, how wrong can you go with a soup? And the answer is both not at all and very! Which is good news and bad news for when you are making soup. It is such a personal thing and these recipes can only give you an idea of flavour combinations and different types of style. The real art is in the final touches – just a little more seasoning, a touch of stock to gain that perfect smoothness without sacrificing on flavour, or perhaps a spoonful of cream to give an underlying richness to the soup.

Nutritionally, soups are an excellent way to achieve the recommended five portions of vegetables and fruit that young and old should be eating every day in order to maintain a healthy diet. Full of fibre, vitamins and minerals, they make a visually colourful palate, an enticingly attractive way of eating your 'greens'.

Freshness and quality are the essentials of a good soup – based on the assumption that any soup is only as good as the ingredients in it. Hence this book is divided by seasons, making use of ingredients when they are most plentiful and their flavour is at its best.

At the end of each chapter are some recipes for suggested accompanments for the soups – breads, muffins, croustades and such like. These will enhance and complement the soups. Do give a little thought to matching the choice of accompaniment with the soup so that they work well together or provide an amicable contrast, thus ensuring that they do not drown out the flavours you have so carefully constructed.

I hope that you will enjoy this book and have fun experimenting with the recipes. They are ideas to spark off your imagination and provide a base from which to develop your own ideas. The ultimate art is knowing how much seasoning to add, or whether a dash of a little something or other would make all the difference. It is what, when you come to taste it, separates a good soup from a great soup!

Basic Principles of Soup Making

There are a number of basic principles to bear in mind when making your own soup; otherwise, the world is your oyster!

Sweating: most recipes start by telling you to 'sweat' the vegetables. Whilst not the most attractive of phrases to use in cookery, it is an accurate description.

The ingredients are gently cooked in a little fat until their juices begin to run, which signals their flavour being drawn out. The pan is covered to help encourage this process by trapping the steam, which in turn helps to soften the vegetables. This is usually done for 10 minutes, with the pan needing to be shaken occasionally to prevent the ingredients sticking to the bottom and subsequently burning. On the whole the ingredients remain colourless in order to give a gentle sweet flavour. Browning the food will achieve a stronger flavour and darker colour as a result of the ingredients caramelising.

Simmering: the main cooking method for soup. The pan is covered to keep in the moisture. Simmering softens the ingredients without harshly tumbling them and expelling all their flavour into the liquid, which results in the vegetables not tasting of much at all.

Sieving: vegetables that tend to be fibrous (such as celery), or have tough skins (peppers and tomatoes) are best sieved to give a pleasing textured soup without any rough bits on the tongue.

Re-heating: a gentle process, without boiling, just to bring the soup up to temperature. If adding single cream it is important not to let the soup boil as this will cause the cream to separate and form a fatty film on the surface.

Freezing: all stocks and many soups freeze well. This makes them a particularly good way of using up a glut of vegetables. Making twice as much as you need also means that you have a useful standby meal for another day.

Quantities: generally, allow an average of 300 ml (½ pint) soup per person.

Tips for Soup Making

Soups are such an individual thing in terms of preference of consistency, strength of flavour and smoothness of texture, that it is difficult to make any hard and fast rules. So here are just a few general tips that I have picked up over the years. I hope you will find them helpful!

INGREDIENTS

Stock – a good stock is the basic requirement of any soup and essential for those that have a mild flavour, such as Fennel, Orange and Sun-dried Tomato Soup (page 53), and cold soups (e.g. Lebanese Chilled Cucumber Soup, page 58). When using dried beans or lentils, make sure that you use a light flavoured or half strength stock, since the long cooking time causes evaporation, which in turn intensifies the flavour.

Seasonality – seasonal vegetables are notably best on two accounts: their flavour is likely to be at its peak and, because they are more plentiful, they are often less expensive to buy. If you are lucky enough to grow your own vegetables, you may well be looking for creative ways in which to use up a glut after the novelty of the precious first harvest is over!

Leeks – these must have been made for soup making! They add a more subtle dimension than onions, so are ideal in soups with a mild flavour, and melt down beautifully as well.

Potatoes – generally floury ones, such as Maris Piper or King Edward, give a good consistency if the soup is going to be liquidised. Do take care with the size you add to a recipe as too much may unintentionally over thicken it, and vice versa. A little more or less stock should rectify this though.

Dried beans – unless you are using a more obscure variety, canned beans save so much time. Remember that they will not absorb so much of the liquid though because they have already been re-hydrated, plus the cooking time is that much shorter. Do add them in time to enable them to absorb the other flavours in the soup though.

Herbs – whether you decide to use fresh or dried is probably dictated by the time of year, availability from your local shops or whether you have them ready to cut outside your kitchen door! As a general rule of thumb, if using dried herbs use about one-third the quantity of fresh.

Spices – spices and herbs are the unsung heroes of soup making – busy beavering away behind the scenes but making the crucial difference to depth of flavour in a soup. Nowadays there are some ready-to-use short cuts available in jars, taking away the need

for tedious preparation. Lemon grass, ginger, chilli, minced garlic, basil and coriander are all available in oils. You can also find jars of curry pastes, which work well in Thai- and Indian-style soups.

Tomatoes – canned chopped tomatoes or passatta (sieved tomatoes) are relatively inexpensive and provide an instant base for tomato soups. If using fresh tomatoes do include their juices. Tough skins are usually removed, and the seeds are preferably left out. Push these, and any attached pulp, through a sieve, and add the strained juices to the soup.

Thickeners – a number of different options are available to thicken soup to the consistency you wish to achieve. Warming, meaty soups work well with a thick starch base of rice, potato or pasta; some soups use a roux; whilst others rely on the addition of cream or egg yolks, which also enrich the liquid.

Toppings – these are the final flourish on your soup, providing colour, texture and flavour. They

can transform a bowl of plain vegetables into a sumptuous soup just by adding a dollop of cream, smattering of nuts or drizzle of flavoured oil. They also provide visual clues as to what flavours the recipient might expect to experience. Hence it is important to echo what is in the soup in the ingredients that you choose for garnishing.

EQUIPMENT
Liquidiser – this is excellent for the job of puréeing soups. It is important not to overfill the jug as hot liquid could spout out from the top and cause a burn. It is therefore advisable to liquidise all the soups in this book in at least two batches.

Food processors – also suitable, although they do tend to chop the ingredients and require a bit more work with using the pulsing action.

Hand held blenders – very good for puréeing small quantities and with the added advantage of saving on washing up as you can purée the soup individually in a large mug or in the saucepan in which it was made.

Stocks

'Stock is the secret of successful soups' should be the mantra for soup making enthusiasts! Home-made stock, suitably flavoured, allows the cook to determine the underlying current, and hence the ultimate taste, of the soup. Subtle variances can be brought about by adding more or different herbs, intensifying the liquid by reducing it and making adjustments to the colour, such as leaving the skins of onions on.

Introduction

It is vital to use stock that you have made yourself for soups that are either to be served cold, or have a subtle flavour that might be lost by the rather harsh flavour of stock cubes or granules. Having said that, stock cubes have their place when you are in a hurry. They are a convenient store cupboard standby, taking up very little storage space, and are not expensive. Tablets of stock cubes and bouillon powders are salty though, so it is best to season your soup at the end of cooking, once you have measured the flavour. Used in robust soups, particularly highly spiced ones, or for everyday cooking, they are both quick and easy to use. For a special occasion though, it is well worth taking the time and trouble to make your own, which will give the finished soup a far superior flavour. After all, stock constitutes the main proportion of a soup. The stock can be made ahead, in double the quantity, and what you are not using can be frozen, in labelled batches, for another time. Generally stock will keep for 3–4 days in the fridge or up to 3 months in the freezer. A compromise is the tubs of fresh stock available from larger supermarkets. These work out to be expensive, especially if you are catering for large numbers, but have a good flavour, thereby making a viable substitute if you are short on time.

In the modern climate of recycling and consciousness about reducing waste it is surprising that there is not more of a move toward making stock from discarded stems of vegetables and carcasses of poultry and meat joints. Perhaps it is an indulgence left over from post-war days that we no longer have to scrimp and save all leftovers or, more probably, a lack of time. It does not take too much trouble when preparing a roast meal to toss the discarded topped and tailed ends from vegetables, liquor drained from their cooking and stripped carcass/bones from the joint into a pot with a few herbs and leave to simmer whilst you relax after an enjoyable meal. Alternatively, off-cuts of meat and bones are available from butchers or supermarkets with fresh meat/fish counters, often for no charge at all. The resulting stock has a far more natural taste, and the added advantage of being more nutritious than the chemically constituted ones.

In this book, each recipe advises which particular type of stock to use. When creating your own soup, think about using the stock that will best enhance the flavour of the ingredients chosen. Taking even only a few simple ingredients, a wonderful soup can be made by using a rich home-made stock that will add body and a depth of flavour unachievable by stock cubes or granules.

Some final advice – from one who has learnt from experience – having taken some time and trouble to conjure up an imaginative soup for a vegetarian friend, think before using chicken in preference to vegetable stock!

Stock Recipes

In this chapter are recipes for the four main types of stock that are used in this book – vegetable, chicken, fish and meat.

BUT FIRSTLY A FEW POINTERS

Always make sure that the vegetables and bones in the pan are just covered with water. Recipes with a longer cooking time may need to have a little more boiling water added to top them up during cooking.

For a more intensely flavoured stock, reduce the liquor by boiling in a pan with a large surface area. Removing the lid makes the evaporation process quicker.

Meat and poultry stocks take longer to cook in order to draw out as much flavour from the bones as possible – attempting to hurry this process by boiling the stock very hard is not a feasible option!

Leeks are a good vegetable to use as the green part of the stem, usually discarded, is just as flavoursome. Parsley stalks are another excellent way of making use of the whole ingredient seeing as most of their flavour is concentrated here.

For a clear stock it is best to disturb the pan as little as possible (apart from skimming off any scum that manifests on the surface). When straining through a sieve at the end of simmering, do not be tempted to try to push the ingredients through to extract any more goodness. It may also be necessary to then strain the stock through a piece of muslin in order to achieve a clear stock, free from impurities.

Only add a small amount of salt and pepper to the stock base ingredients when making. You need to bear in mind that as the liquid reduces, so the flavour intensifies. It is therefore better to season the finished soup, not the stock, as you will have more of an idea how much is needed.

Vegetable Stock

Makes: 1.2 litres (2 pints) *Vegetarian*
Preparation time: *10 minutes + 30 minutes cooking*
Freezing: *recommended*

The finer the vegetables are chopped, the quicker the cooking time! If you require a stock with a more intense flavour, leave the skins on the onions and brown the vegetables in a little butter or oil for about 10 minutes before adding the water and herbs.

1 onion, chopped
1 leek, sliced
2 carrots, sliced
1 stalk celery, sliced
few parsley stalks/sprig of thyme
8–10 black peppercorns
bay leaf
1.5 litres (2½ pints) cold water
pinch salt

1 Put all the ingredients into a large lidded saucepan.

2 Bring slowly to the boil, reduce the heat and simmer, with the lid at an angle, for 30 minutes.

3 Using a large spoon, skim off any scum from the surface as it appears. There is no need to stir the stock.

4 Remove the pan from the heat and pour the contents into a large sieve placed over a bowl. Do not push the vegetables through, but allow the stock to drain naturally.

5 Cool before refrigerating. Keep for up to 3–4 days in the fridge or label and freeze until required.

Chicken Stock

Makes: 1.2 litres (2 pints)
Preparation time: *10 minutes + 2–3 hours cooking*
Freezing: *recommended*

Chicken is probably the stock most often used in soup making because of the roundness of flavour it imparts. It can be made with either inexpensive raw meat (such as wings), or a couple of carcases left over from a roast joint. Freeze the 'skeletons' and when you have a batch, make your stock.

450 g (1 lb) raw chicken wings or 2 large
   chicken carcasses (broken down to fit in
   the pot)
1 onion, chopped
2 carrots, sliced
1 stick celery, sliced
8–10 black peppercorns
handful of parsley stalks/sprig of thyme
bay leaf
2.25 litres (4 pints) cold water
pinch salt

1 Place all the ingredients into a large lidded saucepan.

2 Bring slowly to the boil, reduce the heat and simmer with the lid at an angle for 2–3 hours.

3 Using a large spoon, skim off any scum from the surface as it appears. There is no need to stir the stock.

4 Remove the pan from the heat and pour the contents into a large sieve placed over a bowl. Do not push the ingredients through, but allow the stock to drain naturally.

5 Cool before refrigerating overnight.

6 Remove any fat that has set on the surface and discard.

7 Either keep refrigerated for up to 3–4 days or label and freeze until required.

Tip: Giblets used to be sold in the cavities of chickens. Regulations now no longer allow this, but if you can get hold of some from your butcher then use these as well (without the liver) for a superior flavour.

Fish Stock

Makes: 1.2 litres (2 pints)
Preparation time: *10 minutes + 30 minutes cooking*
Freezing: *recommended*

Ask your fishmonger or at the fresh fish counter in the supermarket for off cuts, heads, bones and trimmings. Make sure that they are from white fish only.

900 g (2 lb) white fish bones and trimmings
1 onion, chopped
2 carrots, sliced
1 leek, sliced
1 stick celery, sliced
few parsley stalks
bay leaf
strip of pared lemon rind
8–10 black peppercorns
1.5 litres (2½ pints) cold water
pinch salt

1 Place all the ingredients into a large lidded saucepan.

2 Bring slowly to the boil, reduce the heat and simmer with the lid at an angle for 30 minutes.

3 Using a large spoon, skim off any scum from the surface as it appears. There is no need to stir the stock.

4 Remove the pan from the heat and pour the contents into a large sieve placed over a bowl. Do not push the ingredients through, but allow the stock to drain naturally.

5 Cool before refrigerating. Keep for 1–2 days in the fridge or label and freeze until required.

Tip: Depending what you intend to use this stock for, a glassful of dry white wine could be added with the water.

Meat Stock

Makes: 1.2 litres (2 pints)
Preparation time: *10 minutes + 1 hour roasting + 3 hours simmering*
Freezing: *recommended*

This recipe can be used for lamb or beef. Roasting the bones and vegetables gives a darker coloured result and stronger flavour. Traditionally beef bones that contain the marrow are prized. You will need to ask the butcher to cut up the bones for you, otherwise they might not fit in the saucepan!

1.35 kg (3 lb) lamb or beef bones and
    trimmings
2 onions, chopped
2 carrots, sliced
2 sticks celery, sliced
2 tomatoes, chopped
handful of parsley stalks/sprig of thyme
bay leaf
8–10 black peppercorns
2.25 litres (4 pints) cold water
pinch salt

1 Pre-heat the oven to Gas Mark 8/
   230°C/450°F.

2 Place the bones and trimmings in a large
   roasting pan. Roast in the oven for
   30 minutes.

3 Remove the pan from the oven, add the
   onions, carrots and celery, baste with fat that
   has come out of the trimmings and cook for a
   further 30 minutes.

4 Using a slotted spoon, transfer the bones
   and vegetables into a large lidded saucepan.
   Reserve the fat to use at another time.

5 Add the tomatoes, herbs, bay leaf, peppercorns,
   water and a pinch of salt to the pan. Bring
   slowly to the boil, reduce the heat and simmer
   with the lid on at an angle for 3 hours, topping
   up with boiling water as necessary.

6 Using a large spoon, skim off any scum from
   the surface as it appears. There is no need to
   stir the stock.

7 Remove the pan from the heat and pour the
   contents into a large sieve placed over a bowl.
   Do not push the ingredients through, but allow
   the stock to drain naturally.

8 Cool before refrigerating. Remove any fat that
   has set on the surface and discard.

9 Keep for up to 3–4 days in the fridge or label
   and freeze until required.

Spring

At last there are signs of new shoots appearing. A sudden lushness to the hedgerows and longer days signal that spring is on its way. Time to make the most of tender young fresh vegetables – broad beans, leeks, brassicas and spinach – whilst savouring the last of winter's potatoes and root vegetables.

Spinach Soup with Chickpeas

Serves: 4
Preparation time: *20 minutes + 35 minutes cooking*
Freezing: *not recommended*

A chunky soup, full of flavour. Serve with Naan Bread with Fennel and Black Onion Seeds (page 138).

1 teaspoon coriander seeds
½ teaspoon cumin seeds
1 tablespoon olive oil
1 onion, chopped
2 cloves garlic, crushed
1 teaspoon turmeric
115 g (4 oz) spinach, washed and roughly torn
410 g can chickpeas, rinsed and drained
4 tomatoes, skinned, de-seeded and roughly
　chopped
600 ml (1 pint) chicken stock (page 15)
juice of ½ lemon
salt
freshly ground black pepper

1 Crush the coriander and cumin seeds using a pestle and mortar.

2 Heat the oil in a large lidded saucepan, add the spices, onion, garlic and turmeric and stir well. Cover and sweat for 10 minutes, shaking the pan occasionally.

3 Stir in the spinach, chickpeas, tomatoes, stock and lemon juice. Bring to the boil, cover and simmer for 20–25 minutes.

4 Cool slightly before puréeing one-third of the soup. Return it to the remaining soup in the pan, stir well, adjust seasoning and heat through.

Greek Style Egg and Lemon Soup with Chicken

Serves: 6
Preparation time: *15 minutes + 1–1½ hours to cook the chicken + 10 minutes for the soup*
Freezing: *not recommended*

A close family friend who now lives and works in Greece gave me the inspiration for this recipe, which somehow uses only a few basic ingredients to achieve a result quite 'out of this world'. In Greece, the egg and lemon base is known as avgolemono.

FOR THE CHICKEN:
1 small/medium chicken
Stock ingredients (roughly chopped onion and carrots, parsley stalks, dried tarragon, bay leaf, black peppercorns, lemon rind and salt)

FOR THE SOUP:
225 g (8 oz) long grain rice, rinsed
3 eggs
juice of 3 lemons
2 tablespoons chopped fresh tarragon
salt
freshly ground black pepper

1 Place the chicken in a large lidded saucepan in which it fits snugly. Pour in enough water to just cover its thighs and add the stock ingredients of your choice. Bring slowly to a simmer, cover and cook for 1–1½ hours, testing to see that the juices run clear after that time.

2 Remove the chicken and, when cool enough to handle, shred the meat into bite-sized pieces.

3 Measure the liquid and make it up to 1.75 litres (3 pints).

4 Bring this to the boil, add the rice and simmer for 10 minutes, until the rice is just cooked.

5 Three minutes before the rice is done, prepare the avgolemono. Whisk the eggs for a couple of minutes until foamy and fluffy. Gradually add in the lemon juice, whisking continuously.

6 Remove the stock from the heat and slowly add a couple of ladles of hot stock from the pan to the avgolemono. Whisk it in. Pour the mixture back into the stock and rice, stirring all the time until it thickens slightly. Do not return to the heat or the soup will curdle.

7 Add as much of the chicken as you need. Stir in the tarragon and season to taste.

8 Serve immediately without re-heating.

Fast Minestrone Soup

Serves: 4–6
Preparation time: *15 minutes + 20 minutes cooking*
Freezing: *not recommended*

A long-term favourite, this variation makes use of quick cooking veggies and pasta, and passatta as a ready-made sauce. Garnish each bowl with a big sprig of basil so that you get a whiff of fragrance each time you bend your head to eat the soup!

1 tablespoon olive oil
2 cloves garlic, crushed
1 onion, chopped
2 carrots, diced
400 g can flageolet beans, rinsed and drained
2 courgettes, sliced
1.2 litres (2 pints) vegetable stock (page 14)
300 ml (½ pint) passatta
2 tablespoons chopped fresh parsley
2 tablespoons chopped fresh basil
1 teaspoon sugar
115 g (4 oz) small pasta
100 g (3½ oz) Serrano/Parma ham
4–6 large sprigs basil
grated Parmesan or Pecorino cheese to serve

1 Heat the oil in a large lidded saucepan. Add the garlic, onion and carrots, cover and sweat for 10 minutes, shaking the pan occasionally.

2 Add the beans, courgettes, stock, passatta, parsley, basil and sugar. Bring to the boil, stir in the pasta, cover and simmer for 10 minutes.

3 Tear the ham into pieces, discarding any fatty bits, and divide between warmed bowls. Ladle the minestrone on top, garnish each with a sprig of basil and hand round a bowl of grated cheese to serve.

Cannellini Soup with Fiery Cherry Tomato Dressing

Serves: 4
Preparation time: *20 minutes + 35 minutes cooking*
Freezing: *recommended for soup but not dressing*

Bean soup tends to have a fairly bland taste. By topping it with tomatoes roasted in garlic and chilli, both the flavour and colour are enhanced. This topping would also be good for any lentil-based soup.

FOR THE SOUP:
1 tablespoon olive oil
1 onion, chopped
2 sticks celery, sliced
2 x 410 g cans cannellini beans, rinsed and drained
600 ml (1 pint) chicken stock (page 15)
1 bay leaf
salt
freshly ground black pepper

FOR THE CHERRY TOMATO DRESSING:
12 cherry tomatoes on the vine
1 clove garlic, thinly sliced
1 red chilli, de-seeded and finely chopped
2 tablespoons olive oil
salt
freshly ground black pepper
1 teaspoon balsamic vinegar
1 tablespoon chopped fresh Continental parsley

1 Heat the oil in a large lidded saucepan, add the onion and celery, stir to coat, cover and sweat for 15 minutes, shaking the pan occasionally.

2 Add the drained beans, chicken stock and bay leaf. Bring to the boil, cover and simmer for 20 minutes.

3 Cool slightly. Remove the bay leaf and liquidise the soup to a smooth purée. Adjust seasoning if necessary.

4 Meanwhile, pre-heat the oven to Gas Mark 6/ 200°C/400°F. Snip the tomato stalks so that there are three tomatoes on each piece. Place in a small roasting tin. Add the garlic and chilli and toss everything in the oil to coat. Season well with salt and pepper. Roast in the oven for about 10 minutes, taking care to brown but not burn the garlic. Remove from the oven and stir in the balsamic vinegar and chopped parsley.

5 Re-heat the soup gently and ladle into warmed bowls. Spoon the roasted tomatoes over each and drizzle with any remaining juices.

Creamy Garden Soup with Herbs

Serves: 4 *Vegetarian*
Preparation time: *15 minutes + 30 minutes cooking*
Freezing: *not recommended*

Packed with spring vegetables, each spoonful of this soup is fresh from the garden! If you grow your own vegetables then adjust the ingredients list accordingly to include whatever vegetables are available.

6 shallots
25 g (1 oz) butter
1 trimmed leek, sliced
1 carrot, sliced
½ bunch spring onions, trimmed, halved and
  sliced lengthways
115 g (4 oz) baby new potatoes, scrubbed
50 g (2 oz) asparagus spears cut into 2.5 cm
  (1 inch) lengths
600 ml (1 pint) vegetable stock (page 14)
80 g (3 oz) baby broad beans
¹/₈ spring cabbage, shredded
80 g (3 oz) mascarpone
2 tablespoons chopped fresh chervil or
  parsley
2 tablespoons snipped fresh chives
salt
freshly ground black pepper

1 To prepare the shallots, place them in a small bowl, pour over boiling water and leave for 1 minute. Drain and run under cold water, then peel as for onions. Halve them from top to tail.

2 Melt the butter in a large lidded saucepan; add the shallots, leek and carrot. Cover and sweat for 10 minutes, shaking the pan occasionally.

3 Add the spring onions, potatoes, asparagus and vegetable stock. Bring to the boil, cover and simmer for 15 minutes.

4 Stir in the broad beans and cabbage and simmer for just a couple more minutes.

5 Stir through the mascarpone and herbs. Taste and adjust seasoning accordingly.

Carrot and Coriander Soup

Serves: 4
Preparation time: *15 minutes + 40 minutes cooking*
Freezing: *recommended*

This soup is delicious served sprinkled with a little Dukkah (page 44).

25 g (1 oz) butter
450 g (1lb) carrots, sliced
1 onion, chopped
2 teaspoons ground coriander
2 teaspoons freshly grated ginger
1 teaspoon cumin seeds
700 ml (1¼ pints) chicken stock (page 15)
25 g (1 oz) coriander, stalks and leaves
    chopped
1 teaspoon sugar
salt
freshly ground black pepper

1 Melt the butter in a large lidded saucepan; add the carrots, onion, coriander, ginger and cumin seeds. Cover and sweat for 10 minutes to soften.

2 Stir in the stock, coriander and sugar. Bring to the boil and simmer for 30 minutes.

3 Cool slightly then whizz to a smooth purée in a liquidiser. Adjust seasoning.

4 Return the soup to the rinsed out pan and re-heat until piping hot. Serve in warmed bowls garnished with a smattering of Dukkah (page 44).

Spring Risotto Soup

Serves: 6 *Vegetarian*
Preparation time: *15 minutes + 50 minutes cooking*
Freezing: *not recommended*

Make use of early, tender spring vegetables while they have the sweetest flavour. This is a meal in itself, beautifully creamy and made fragrant by the basil.

25 g (1 oz) butter
1 bulb fennel, thinly sliced
6 shallots, sliced
1 clove garlic, crushed
175 g (6 oz) Arborio rice
125 ml (4 fl oz) dry white wine
175 g (6 oz) button mushrooms, halved
1.2 litres (2 pints) hot vegetable stock
   (page 14)
225 g (8 oz) shelled, young broad beans
80 g (3 oz) grated Parmesan cheese
175 g (6 oz) mascarpone
good handful of basil leaves, torn
salt
freshly ground black pepper

1 Melt the butter in a large lidded saucepan, add the fennel, shallots and garlic, cover and sweat for 20 minutes, shaking the pan occasionally.

2 Add the rice and stir for about a minute to coat with the butter.

3 Pour in the wine and let it bubble for a couple of minutes.

4 Stir in the mushrooms and a little of the hot stock. Simmer gently; adding a little more stock as each addition is absorbed. This will take about 25 minutes.

5 Five minutes before all the stock has been used, add the broad beans.

6 Stir through the Parmesan, mascarpone and basil. Check the seasoning; you probably won't need any salt because of the Parmesan. Serve at once, otherwise the soup will thicken on standing.

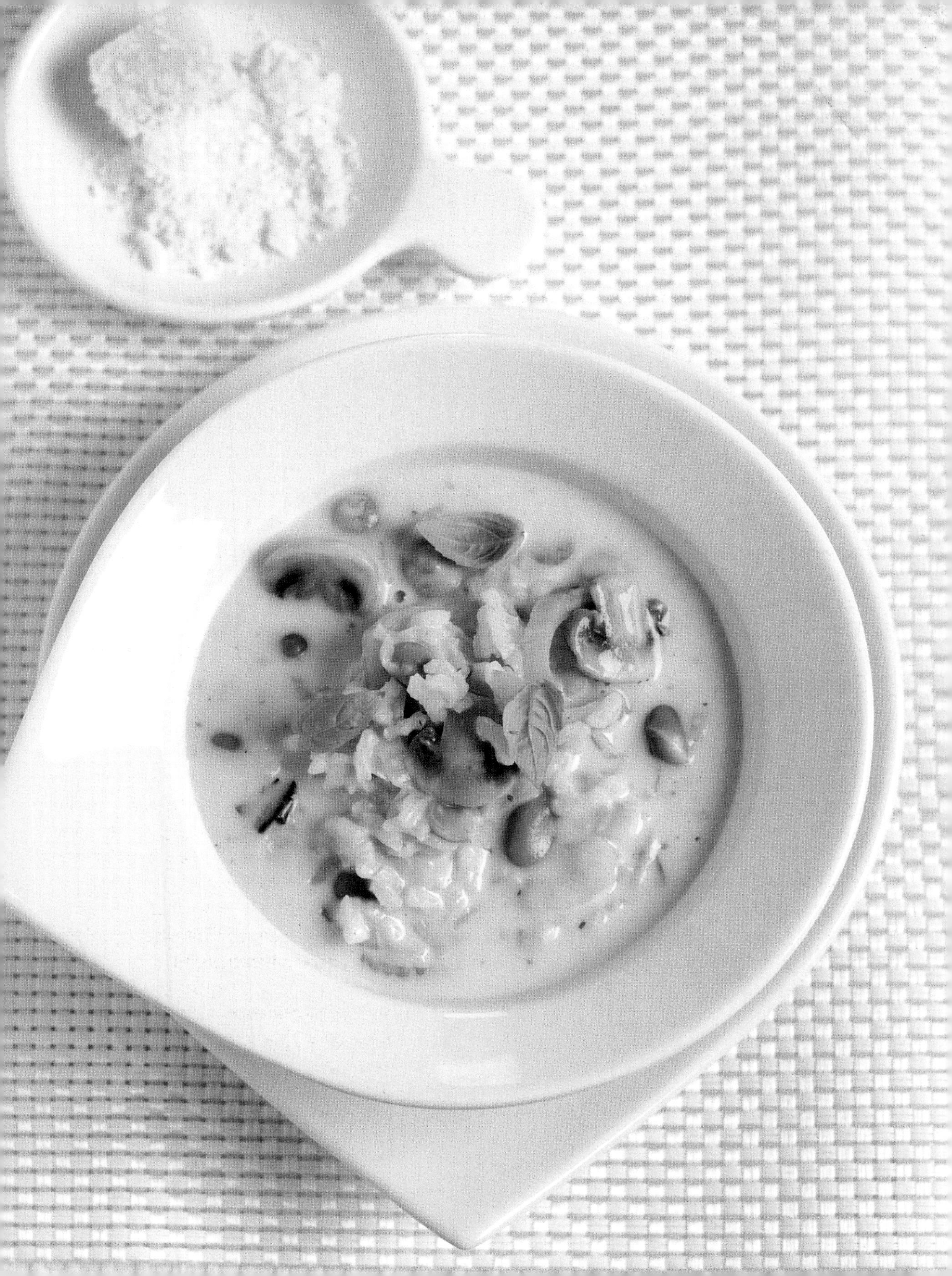

Green Thai Cauliflower Soup

Serves: 4
Preparation time: *15 minutes + 40 minutes cooking*
Freezing: *recommended*

There are numerous Thai pastes available that make excellent quick and easy soup bases, cutting out the need for purchasing an assortment of herbs and spices and having to prepare them.

1 tablespoon oil
1 onion, chopped
1 tablespoon Thai green curry paste
400 ml can coconut milk
300 ml (½ pint) chicken stock (page 15)
1 medium/large potato, diced
1 medium cauliflower, broken into florets
50 g (2 oz) French type beans, trimmed to
   3 cm (1¼ inch)

FOR THE GARNISH:
strips of spring onion
coriander leaves

1 Heat the oil in a large lidded saucepan, add the onion, cover and sweat for 10 minutes, shaking the pan occasionally.

2 Stir in the paste and cook for 1 minute.

3 Add the coconut milk, stock and potato. Bring to the boil, stir in the cauliflower, cover and simmer for 15 minutes.

4 Add the beans and simmer for a further 2–3 minutes.

5 Cool the soup slightly. Purée half the cauliflower florets and about one-third of the liquid. Return to the pan, stir in and heat through.

6 Serve in warmed bowls topped with thin strips of spring onion and coriander leaves.

Parsley Soup

Serves: 4 *Vegetarian*
Preparation time: *15 minutes + 35–40 minutes cooking*
Freezing: *recommended*

This soup always reminds me of the Beatrix Potter stories with Peter Rabbit nibbling on Mr. McGregor's prize parsley and other vegetables!

25 g (1 oz) butter
1 Spanish onion, roughly chopped
1 large potato, diced
2 sticks celery, sliced
2 x 80 g (3 oz) bunches parsley
850 ml (1½ pints) vegetable stock (page 14)
salt
freshly ground black pepper
4 tablespoons single cream for serving

1 Melt the butter in a large lidded saucepan, add the onion, potato and celery, stir to coat. Cover and sweat for 10 minutes, shaking the pan occasionally.

2 Cut the stalks off the parsley and add to the pan with the stock. Simmer, covered, for 20–25 minutes.

3 Stir in the parsley leaves, reserving a few for a garnish, and cook for another 2–3 minutes, until the parsley has wilted down.

4 Allow the soup to cool a little before puréeing in a liquidiser. Sieve to give a smoother consistency.

5 Rinse out the pan. Return the soup to the hob and re-heat gently to just below simmering point. Adjust seasoning.

6 Pour into warmed bowls and serve finished with a swirl of cream and a sprinkle of extra parsley if wished.

Rolling Chicken Broth

Serves: 4–6
Preparation time: *10 minutes + 35 minutes cooking*
Freezing: *not recommended*

Thus called as all the ingredients are tossed in succession into a pan of simmering, fragrant, Oriental-flavoured stock. Kohlrabi has a slightly coconut-like flavour and its crisp texture is perfect for this soup.

FOR THE STOCK:
1.3 litres (2¼ pints) water
50 g (2 oz) fresh coriander
6 spring onions
2 cloves garlic, sliced
2 stalks lemon grass, bruised
1 tablespoon freshly grated ginger

FOR THE SOUP:
1 medium kohlrabi, thickly peeled and cut into
　julienne strips
2 medium carrots, peeled and cut into julienne
　strips
2 tablespoons soy sauce
fingertip of hot chilli in sunflower oil
175 g (6 oz) cooked chicken, torn into strips
80 g (3 oz) mushrooms, sliced

FOR THE GARNISH:
1 teaspoon butter
2 eggs, lightly beaten
25 g (1 oz) salted peanuts, chopped

1　Begin by making the stock. Pour the water into a large lidded saucepan. Trim the stalks from the coriander and add these to the pan. Roughly chop the leaves and reserve.

2　Trim the spring onions and add the trimmings to the stock. Diagonally slice the remaining onions and reserve.

3　Stir in the garlic, whole lemon grass and ginger. Bring to the boil, cover and simmer for 30 minutes. Strain and reserve the liquor.

4　Rinse out the pan and return the stock to it. Bring to the boil and add the kohlrabi, carrots, soy sauce and chilli. Simmer for 3 minutes.

5　Toss in the chicken, mushrooms, most of the coriander leaves and the sliced spring onion. Simmer for a further 2 minutes.

6　Meanwhile, melt half the butter in an omelette pan and make a thin omelette with the beaten eggs. Turn out onto a board, roll up loosely and slice thinly into ribbons.

7　Wipe out the pan and melt the remaining butter. Brown the peanuts and set to one side.

8　Ladle the soup into warmed bowls and garnish with the egg ribbons, chopped peanuts and last of the coriander leaves.

Baby Leaf Spinach Soup

Serves: 6 *Vegetarian*
Preparation time: *20 minutes + 25 minutes cooking*
Freezing: *not recommended*

Simple and delicious! This is a quick and easy way to make use of a glut of spinach. Serve garnished with Croûtons (page 48).

2 tablespoons butter
2 trimmed leeks, sliced
2 medium potatoes, peeled and diced
450 g (1 lb) baby spinach leaves, washed
850 ml (1½ pints) vegetable stock (page 14)
good squeeze of lemon juice
¼ freshly grated nutmeg
freshly ground black pepper
salt

FOR THE GARNISH:
Croûtons (page 48)
2 tablespoons toasted pine nuts

1 Melt the butter in a large lidded saucepan. Add the leeks and potatoes, cover and sweat for 10 minutes, shaking the pan occasionally.

2 Stir in the spinach, stock, lemon juice, nutmeg and a grinding of black pepper. Bring to the boil, cover and simmer for 15 minutes.

3 Cool slightly before puréeing.

4 Return to the rinsed pan and re-heat gently until piping hot. Adjust seasoning and serve sprinkled with toasted pine nuts and Croûtons.

Cuban Style Fish Soup

Serves: 4
Preparation time: *10 minutes + 30–35 minutes cooking*
Freezing: *not recommended*

This soup is unusual in that it is thickened with ground almonds. It also uses sweet paprika, which I have unashamedly used in a few of these soup recipes – it gives a warming feel to the back of the throat and is a great secret ingredient standby for the hardy soup maker!

1 tablespoon olive oil
1 Spanish onion, thinly sliced
1 red pepper, de-seeded and diced
1 clove garlic, crushed
400 g can chopped tomatoes
600 ml (1 pint) fish stock (page 16)
150 ml (¼ pint) dry white wine
1 teaspoon soft brown sugar
¼ teaspoon smoked paprika
1 bay leaf
salt
80 g (3 oz) ground almonds, toasted
225 g (½ lb) cod fillet, skinned
freshly ground black pepper
4 bay leaves to garnish

1 Heat the oil in a large lidded saucepan. Add the onion, pepper and garlic, cover and sweat for 15–20 minutes until softened. Shake the pan occasionally.

2 Stir in the tomatoes, stock, wine, sugar, paprika and bay leaf. Season with salt. Bring to the boil, cover and simmer for 10 minutes.

3 Stir through the ground almonds and lay the cod fillet, either in a whole piece or halved if it doesn't fit in the pan, on top of the soup. Bring to a gentle simmer, cover and steam the fish for 5–6 minutes, or until just cooked through.

4 Remove the bay leaf and season soup to taste. Divide fish and soup between warmed serving bowls and serve at once, each garnished with a fresh bay leaf.

Tip: Serve this soup with plenty of crusty bread to mop up the juices.

Spicy Parsnip Soup

Serves: 4
Preparation time: *15 minutes + 40 minutes cooking*
Freezing: *recommended*

This soup has been around for a while, and there's a reason for that – the old ones are the best. Below is my version.

50 g (2 oz) butter
1 medium onion, chopped
450 g (1 lb) parsnips, cored and chopped
2 teaspoons medium curry powder
2 teaspoons freshly grated ginger
600 ml (1 pint) chicken stock (page 15)
1 medium Bramley apple, peeled, cored and
  grated
300 ml (½ pint) milk
squeeze of lemon juice
salt
freshly ground black pepper

1 Melt the butter in a large lidded saucepan; add the onion and parsnips. Stir in the curry powder and ginger, cover and sweat for 10 minutes, shaking the pan occasionally.

2 Add the stock and simmer for 20 minutes.

3 Stir the apple into the soup. Continue to cook for a further 10 minutes.

4 Cool slightly. Pour into a liquidiser with the milk and lemon juice. Purée until smooth and season to taste.

5 Return to the pan and heat through gently, without boiling, until piping hot. Serve at once.

Tip: Garnish with Parsnip Crisps (page 49) or a julienne of green/red eating apples.

Broccoli and Melted Gruyère Soup

Serves: 4
Preparation time: *5 minutes + 22 minutes cooking*
Freezing: *not recommended*

Broccoli needs to be cooked for just long enough to soften the stalks without the florets becoming soggy. Therefore make sure that the stalks are submerged in the stock whilst cooking. Using the cooking liquid in the soup helps make sure that none of the valuable vitamins have a chance to escape!

25 g (1 oz) butter
1 onion, chopped
425 ml (¾ pint) chicken stock (page 15)
350 g (12 oz) broccoli, including the stalks
2 tablespoons flour
150 ml (¼ pint) milk
80 g (3 oz) grated Gruyère cheese
good pinch of nutmeg
salt
freshly ground black pepper

1 Melt the butter in a large lidded saucepan, add the onion, cover and sweat for 10 minutes, shaking the pan occasionally.

2 Meanwhile, bring the stock to the boil in a second pan and simmer the broccoli for 10 minutes.

3 Stir the flour into the onion mixture and cook for 1–2 minutes. Gradually blend in the milk to make a smooth, thick sauce. Add the Gruyère and stir until melted.

4 Reserve a large floret of broccoli and the cooking liquid. Plunge the rest of the broccoli into cold water to prevent it cooking any further. Drain and stir into white sauce with the cooking liquid. Season with nutmeg, salt and pepper.

5 Cool the mixture slightly and purée in a blender until smooth and creamy.

6 Return the soup to the rinsed pan and heat through gently (the cheese tends to toughen if it is overcooked). Divide between warmed bowls and garnish with small pieces of broccoli floret.

Carrot and Orange Soup

Serves: 4–6 *Vegetarian*
Preparation time: *15 minutes + 45 minutes cooking*
Freezing: *recommended*

Bright and fresh as spring itself — a taste of the summer to come!

25 g (1 oz) butter
900 g (2 lb) carrots, sliced
2 trimmed leeks, sliced
850 ml (1½ pints) vegetable stock (page 14)
zest of 1 orange
juice of 2 oranges
2 teaspoons sugar
salt
freshly ground black pepper

FOR THE GARNISH:
zest of ½ orange
handful chopped fresh parsley

1 Melt the butter in a large lidded saucepan, add the carrots and leeks, cover and sweat for 10 minutes, shaking the pan occasionally.

2 Blend in the stock, orange zest and juice and the sugar. Bring to simmering point, cover and bubble gently for 30 minutes, until the carrot is cooked through.

3 Meanwhile prepare the garnish. Peel strips of rind from the orange and pare away any white pith, which will make it sour. Slice the rind very thinly into strips. Place these in a cup and pour over boiling water to just cover. Leave for 30 seconds, drain and plunge into cold water to prevent any further cooking.

4 Cool the soup slightly before puréeing in a liquidiser until smooth. Adjust seasoning to taste.

5 Return the soup to the rinsed out pan and re-heat gently. Divide between warmed serving bowls and garnish with the julienne of orange and a sprinkling of chopped parsley.

Photo: For Croûtons see page 48.

West Country Soup

Serves: 4
Preparation time: *15 minutes + 35 minutes cooking*
Freezing: *recommended prior to adding cream*

Although this soup is quite rich, toss some grated Gruyère with torn bread Croûtons (page 48) to finish off – the cheese melts into the soup and **the croûtons give it a lovely crunch.**

25 g (1 oz) butter
1 large leek, sliced
1 medium carrot, sliced
2 medium potatoes, peeled and sliced
150 ml (¼ pint) cider
425 ml (¾ pint) chicken stock (page 15)
2 sprigs sage
4 tablespoons single cream
salt
freshly ground black pepper

FOR THE GARNISH:
50 g (2 oz) grated Gruyère cheese
torn bread Croûtons (page 48)

1 Melt the butter in a large lidded saucepan. Add the leek, carrot and potatoes, stir to coat, cover and sweat for 10 minutes. Shake the pan occasionally.

2 Stir in the cider, stock and sage. Bring to the boil, cover and bubble gently for 25 minutes until the vegetables are tender.

3 Cool the soup slightly. Remove the sage leaves and discard. Purée the soup to a lovely smooth consistency.

4 Return to the rinsed out pan, stir in the cream and season. Re-heat carefully, without boiling.

5 Serve topped with the cheese and Croûtons.

Split Pea, Leek and Ham Soup

Serves: 4

Preparation time: *overnight soaking + 15 minutes + 40 minutes cooking*

Freezing: *recommended*

A thick, old-fashioned soup; short on colour but long on flavour.

125 g (4 oz) dried yellow split peas
1 tablespoon olive oil
3 trimmed leeks, sliced
1 onion, chopped
850 ml (1½ pints) ham or vegetable stock
   (page 14)
2 tablespoons chopped fresh parsley
80 g (3 oz) cooked ham, diced
salt
freshly ground black pepper

FOR THE GARNISH:
handful chopped fresh parsley
50 g (2 oz) diced ham

1 Soak the peas overnight in cold water. Drain, rinse and put into a saucepan with fresh water. Boil rapidly, uncovered, for 10 minutes, then drain.

2 Whilst the peas are cooking, heat the oil in a large lidded saucepan, add the leeks and onion, cover and sweat for 10 minutes, shaking the pan occasionally.

3 Add the peas to the vegetables, together with the stock and parsley. Bring to the boil, cover and simmer for 20 minutes. Stir in the ham and cook for a further 10 minutes.

4 Cool slightly and purée until smooth, adding a little more stock if necessary for the desired consistency.

5 Re-heat the soup and ladle into warmed bowls. Scatter with parsley and ham and serve.

Dukkah

Serves: 4 *Vegetarian/Vegan*
Preparation time: *5 minutes +10 minutes cooking*
Freezing: *not recommended*

This is an Egyptian snack traditionally served with pitta bread, which is brushed with melted butter and dunked in the dukkah. It is also used as a coating for meats. Serve a scattering over each bowl of soup for an added flavour dimension. Tomato-based soups are good with dukkah, as are carrot soups.

50 g (2 oz) blanched almonds, hazelnuts or pistachios
2 teaspoons coriander seeds
2 teaspoons sesame seeds
1 teaspoon cumin seeds
1/8 teaspoon coarse sea salt
1/4 teaspoon dried thyme

1 Pre-heat the oven to Gas Mark 4/ 180°C/350°F.

2 Spread the nuts and seeds on a baking tray and roast in the oven for approximately 10 minutes until golden. Keep an eye on them and shake the tray occasionally.

3 Grind the salt in a large pestle and mortar. Add the toasted ingredients and pound to small pieces. A blender may be used to do this, but take care not to over process otherwise the nuts may let out some oil.

4 Stir in the thyme and leave to cool. Store in an airtight container.

Cornbread with Spring Onion and Chilli

Serves: 8 *Vegetarian*
Preparation time: *15 minutes + 20–25 minutes baking*
Freezing: *recommended*

This recipe is made to go with soup – while the soup simmers the cornbread has time to bake – the perfect partnership!

50 g (2 oz) butter
1 bunch spring onions, thinly sliced
1 red chilli, de-seeded and finely chopped
175 g (6 oz) yellow cornmeal/polenta
115 g (4 oz) plain flour
1 tablespoon baking powder
1 tablespoon sugar
½ teaspoon coarse sea salt
freshly ground black pepper
250 ml (8 fl oz) milk
2 eggs, beaten

1 Pre-heat the oven to Gas Mark 6/ 200°C/400°F. Grease and base line a 20 x 20 cm (8 x 8 inch) shallow tin.

2 Melt the butter in a pan, add the spring onions and chilli and cook for 2–3 minutes to soften. Allow to cool slightly.

3 Combine the cornmeal, flour, baking powder, sugar, salt and pepper in a bowl. Make a well in the centre.

4 Pour the milk, eggs and melted butter mixture into the well. Stir to make a smooth batter.

5 Pour into the prepared tin, spreading to the edges. Bake for 20–25 minutes until risen and golden.

6 Turn out onto a wire rack and serve the same day, hot or cold, cut into squares.

3-in-1 Bread

Serves: 12 *Vegetarian*
Preparation time: *30 minutes + 1¾ hours proving + 25–30 minutes baking*
Freezing: *not recommended*

This bread came about because I had several bread toppings that I wanted to use, so I amalgamated them all into one giant tray bake loaf.

FOR THE DOUGH:
450 g (1 lb) strong white flour
1 teaspoon coarse sea salt
1 packet easy blend yeast
2 tablespoons olive oil
300 ml (½ pint) warm water

FOR THE SOUR CREAM AND ONION TOPPING:
2 teaspoons butter
1 small onion, thinly sliced into rings
salt
freshly ground black pepper
3 tablespoons soured cream

FOR THE PARMESAN AND SUN-DRIED TOMATO TOPPING:
2 halves sun-dried tomato in oil, snipped
a little sun-dried tomato oil for brushing
2 tablespoons grated Parmesan cheese

FOR THE GARLIC AND ROSEMARY TOPPING:
1 tablespoon softened butter
½ clove garlic, crushed
tender sprig ends of rosemary

1 Make the bread. Combine the flour, salt and yeast in a large bowl. Add the oil and water and mix to a soft dough. Turn out onto a work surface and knead for 10 minutes (5 minutes in a machine) until soft and smooth, adding more flour only if necessary.

2 Place the dough in an oiled polythene bag and leave to prove in a warm place for about an hour.

3 Make the onion topping next as this needs to cool. Melt the butter in a pan, add the onion and fry for about 5 minutes, stirring occasionally, until transparent and soft. Season and leave to cool.

4 Grease a roasting tin measuring at least 23 x 28 cm (9 x 11 inches).

5 Cut 40 g (1½ oz) off the dough and leave in the bag for the moment. Using your knuckles, press the remainder evenly into the prepared tin. Then take the reserved dough and divide into two. Roll each piece out very thinly into a pencil shape, twice the width of the tin (i.e. 46 cm/18 inches) long. Fold one piece at the halfway point, and twist to form a kind of plait. Repeat with the remaining piece. Lay these across the width of the dough to divide it into three sections. Brush with a little water to secure.

6 Press the pieces of sun-dried tomato firmly into the first section of dough (otherwise they do have a tendency to burn!) Brush with a little of the oil and sprinkle with the Parmesan.

7 Next, scatter the onions over the centre third. Dollop teaspoonfuls of the soured cream on top, making sure that the onion is not completely covered, as this will allow it to turn golden.

8 For the final third, combine the butter and garlic, spread over the surface of the dough and push sprigs of rosemary into it.

9 Return the tin to the oiled bag and prove for 30–45 minutes, until doubled in size.

10 Pre-heat the oven to Gas Mark 5/ 190°C/375°F.

11 Bake the bread just above the middle of the oven for 25–30 minutes. Allow it to cool a little on a wire rack before serving warm.

Tip: This is great for a group of friends – present it at the table in all its glory and invite everyone to cut off pieces of their favourite flavoured sections!

Croûtons

Serves: 4 *Vegetarian/Vegan*
Preparation time: *5 minutes + 10 minutes baking*
Freezing: *not recommended*

This is one garnish that has withstood the trends of years, albeit having subtly evolved from cubes of sliced, crustless bread to the now more widely used Ciabatta-based squares.

about 1/6 Ciabatta loaf, diced into 1 cm
   (½ inch) cubes
1 tablespoon olive oil

1   Pre-heat the oven to Gas Mark 6/ 200°C/400°F.

2   Place the bread cubes in a bowl. Drizzle with the olive oil. Mix well to coat.

3   Turn the cubes onto a baking sheet and cook in the centre of the oven for about 10 minutes, checking regularly to make sure that they don't burn – you're aiming for a golden colour.

4   If not using immediately, cool on the baking sheet and store in an airtight container for up to 3 days. Re-heat for a few minutes in the oven before using to garnish your soup.

Tips: As a general rule, allow 50 g (2 oz) bread per person.

It is probably easiest to bake the bread in the oven, rather than trying to obtain an even colour by frying. Olive oil or butter both taste good. Ring the changes by flavouring the oil with garlic, adding a sprinkle of herbs, mixing the cubes with pesto or sprinkling with sesame seeds, depending what best compliments your soup.

Day-old bread works well, particularly the continental country loaves. Aim to cut the bread into 1 cm (½ inch) cubes. Alternatively, just tear the bread into small pieces for a more rustic appearance.

Illustration on page 41

Parsnip Crisps

Serves: 4 *Vegetarian/Vegan*
Preparation time: *10 minutes + 20 minutes baking*
Freezing: *not recommended*

These are a great hand round with fairly substantial soups where a bread accompaniment would be too much.

1 medium parsnip
1 tablespoon olive oil
sea salt
freshly ground black pepper

1 Pre-heat the oven to Gas Mark 6/
200°C/400°F.

2 Peel the parsnip and then, using a vegetable
peeler, scrape thin wafers lengthways down
the parsnip. Keep going until you come to the
inner core and discard this.

3 Place the strips of parsnip in a bowl and
drizzle over a little olive oil to just coat.

4 Spread out on a baking tray and season lightly
with salt and pepper.

5 Cook on the top shelf of the oven for about
20 minutes. After 10 minutes you will need
to turn them over – moving the better done
ones at the edge to the centre. Return to the
oven and keep a close check on them as they
burn easily. When crisp, carefully use a slice
to transfer them onto some kitchen paper to
cool.

6 Serve the same day.

Summer

British summers provide scope for an extensive range of seasonal soups. From simple, no-cook varieties for all those sweltering, scorching days when it is too hot to be cooking and appetites are easily satisfied. To the other end of the spectrum – rainy, cool and timeless days when a warming bowl of soup is just what is needed.

Cream of Asparagus Soup

Serves: 4
Preparation time: *15 minutes + 40 minutes cooking + chilling time*
Freezing: *recommended before adding cream*

Quintessentially English, this chilled soup has a distinctive yet delicate flavour.

450 g (1 lb) asparagus spears
850 ml (1½ pints) chicken stock (page 15)
25 g (1 oz) butter
1 bunch spring onions, trimmed and sliced
2 tablespoons plain flour
125 ml (4 fl oz) single cream
salt
freshly ground black pepper

1 Cut the tips from the asparagus spears and cook them in the stock for 5 minutes. Using a slotted spoon, scoop out the tips and plunge them into cold water to refresh. Keep them to one side.

2 Cut the remaining asparagus stalks into smallish pieces.

3 Heat the butter in a large lidded saucepan, toss in the asparagus stalks and spring onions and sweat for 10 minutes, shaking the pan occasionally.

4 Stir in the flour and cook for 1–2 minutes. Gradually blend in the stock. Bring to the boil, cover and simmer gently for 20 minutes.

5 Cool the soup and purée. Sieve it if the asparagus is a bit old and woody.

6 Stir in the cream and adjust seasoning. Then refrigerate for at least a couple of hours until well chilled. (You can put some serving bowls in the fridge at the same time to make sure that everything is very cold!)

7 To serve, stir in most of the asparagus tips, then ladle the soup into bowls and arrange the remaining tips on top.

Fennel, Orange and Sun-dried Tomato Soup

Serves: 6 *Vegetarian/Vegan*
Preparation time: *20 minutes + 40 minutes cooking*
Freezing: *not recommended*

The taste of summer really comes through in this light soup, which makes an ideal starter.

2 tablespoons olive oil
2 small bulbs fennel, thinly sliced
2 trimmed leeks, thinly sliced
2 sticks celery, thinly sliced
80 g (3 oz) sun-dried tomatoes in oil, snipped
pared rind of 1 orange
juice of 2 oranges
850 ml (1½ pints) vegetable stock (page 14)
300 ml (½ pint) dry white wine
salt
freshly ground black pepper

FOR THE GARNISH:
fennel fronds
julienne of orange (see Carrot and Orange
   Soup, page 40)

1 Heat the oil in a large lidded saucepan. Add the fennel, leeks and celery. Stir well to coat, cover and sweat for 20 minutes (fennel takes a while to soften), shaking the pan occasionally.

2 Add the sun-dried tomatoes, pared rind (free from any bitter white pith), orange juice, stock and white wine. Bring to the boil, cover and simmer for 20 minutes.

3 Cool slightly. Remove the orange rind and liquidise the soup to a purée. Adjust seasoning.

4 This soup can be served hot or well chilled, scattered with fronds of fennel and julienne orange strips.

Green Pea and Mint Soup

Serves: 4
Preparation time: *15 minutes + 20 minutes cooking*
Freezing: *recommended prior to adding cream*

This soup has a lovely fresh green colour and can be served hot or cold. When cold it has a mousse-like texture. Fresh or frozen peas work equally well.

2 tablespoons olive oil
2 onions, chopped
115 g (4 oz) potatoes, chopped
450 g (1 lb) shelled peas
600 ml (1 pint) chicken stock (page 15)
leaves from 3 sprigs mint
100 ml (3½ fl oz) single cream
salt
freshly ground black pepper

Tip: For a chic starter, or a hand-round at a drinks party, serve the soup in espresso cups very well chilled and topped with a shot of single cream and pea shoot tips.

1 Heat the oil in a large lidded saucepan, add the onions and potatoes, cover and sweat for 10 minutes, shaking the pan occasionally.

2 Add the peas, stock and mint leaves, bring to the boil, reduce the heat and cover. Simmer for 10 minutes.

3 Cool slightly before puréeing in a liquidiser.

4 Stir in the cream and season to taste.

5 Either chill very well or re-heat to serve hot.

Spring Onion and Lettuce Soup

Serves: 4
Preparation time: *15 minutes + 25 minutes cooking + chilling time*
Freezing: *not recommended*

Fresh in colour and taste, this is the allotment gardener's staple in the summer months when lettuce grows like a weed.

2 tablespoons olive oil
1 bunch spring onions, sliced
225 g (8 oz) potatoes, cubed
425 ml (¾ pint) chicken stock (page 15)
450 g (1 lb) sweet lettuce, such as Romaine or
　Cos, washed
1 teaspoon sugar
4 tablespoons single cream
salt
freshly ground black pepper
Croûtons (page 48) to garnish

1　Heat the butter in a large lidded saucepan, add the spring onions and stir them around in the pan for 2–3 minutes to soften.

2　Add the potatoes and stock, bring to the boil, cover and simmer for 15 minutes, or until the potato softens.

3　Discard the stalks from the lettuce and shred the reminder. Turn up the heat and gradually add the lettuce to the pan, giving it time to wilt down between each addition. Stir in the sugar.

4　Cool the soup slightly before liquidising to a smooth consistency. Add the cream and blitz for a few seconds. Adjust seasoning and chill.

5　Divide the soup between cold serving bowls. Add a couple of ice cubes to each and garnish with Croûtons.

Tip: Serve this delicately flavour soup with Pistachio and Pecorino Biscotti (page 78), spread with a thick layer of cream cheese.

Chilled Watermelon Soup

Serves: 4 *Vegetarian*
Preparation time: *10 minutes + chilling time*
Freezing: *recommended*

When it's hot outside, you don't want to be cooking. This refreshing soup provides an instant answer – it's not even necessary to remove the rather tedious seeds from the watermelon first – sieving will do this.

1 small/medium watermelon, flesh weighing
   approximately 1.35 kg (3 lb)
4 teaspoons chopped fresh oregano
4 teaspoons lime juice
ice cubes
175 g (6 oz) Feta cheese, crumbled

FOR THE GARNISH:
oregano leaves
wedges of lime

1 Cut the watermelon flesh into cubes. Place into a food processor with the oregano and pulse until smooth. Do not over process or it will become very frothy!

2 Pour the pulp through a sieve into a large bowl with a lip. Push as much pulp through as possible – the whole seeds will be left behind. Flavour with lime juice. Chill for at least 2 hours, together with your serving bowls.

3 Put a couple of ice cubes into each chilled bowl and pour over the soup. Heap the Feta into a mound in the centre of each serving and garnish with the oregano leaves and wedges of lime.

Lebanese Chilled Cucumber Soup

Serves: 4–6
Preparation time: *15 minutes + chilling time*
Freezing: *not recommended*

Serve this lovely soup topped with grated egg and prawns to make a light and refreshing main course for the summer months. The soup needs to chill for a couple of hours for two reasons: to make sure that it is really cold, and to give the flavours a chance to blend together. It is best eaten on the day of making.

1 cucumber
80 g (3 oz) cocktail gherkins
2 tablespoons capers, drained
leaves from 4 sprigs mint
1 clove garlic
500 g (1 lb 2 oz) Greek yogurt
175 ml (6 fl oz) chilled vegetable stock
    (page 14)
salt
2 hard boiled eggs, peeled and grated
80 g (3 oz) cooked prawns, shelled
dill or fennel fronds

1 Cut the cucumber in half lengthways and scoop out the seeds. Either grate or dice it very finely.

2 Chop the gherkins, capers, mint and garlic very finely. A blender is good for this. Stir into the cucumber.

3 Add the yogurt and enough stock to give the desired consistency. Season with salt. Cover and refrigerate for a couple of hours.

4 Serve in very cold bowls and garnish with the egg, prawns and dill or fennel fronds.

Thick Roasted Mediterranean Vegetable Soup

Serves: 6 *Vegetarian/Vegan*
Preparation time: *20 minutes + 35–45 minutes cooking*
Freezing: *recommended*

This is a deliciously thick summer soup, making use of the plentiful supply of peppers, courgettes, tomatoes and aubergines at this time of year. It actually originated as a salad, which my mother had made in large quantities. The result the next day – delicious soup!

2 aubergines, quartered and sliced
2 large courgettes, cut into thick slices
2 red peppers, de-seeded and cut into chunks
2 red onions, cut into wedges
900 g (2 lb) tomatoes, skinned, deseeded and
   chopped
1 head garlic, broken into cloves, papery skin
   removed
2 sprigs rosemary
5 tablespoons olive oil
salt
freshly ground black pepper
1.2 litres (2 pints) vegetable stock (page 14)
1 teaspoon balsamic vinegar

1 Pre-heat the oven to Gas Mark 8/ 230°C/450°F.

2 Spread the vegetables, garlic and rosemary on to a large roasting tray. Sprinkle with oil, salt and pepper and give everything a good mix. Arrange in a single layer.

3 Roast on the highest shelf in the oven for 30–35 minutes. Turn the vegetables half way through cooking.

4 Remove the rosemary. Allow to cool slightly before pulsing in batches in a food processor. I like to still be able to identify the vegetables, in which case leave them fairly coarse. This also makes the soup more colourful.

5 Place the vegetables in a large saucepan. Stir in the stock and balsamic vinegar. Bring to the boil and bubble for 5–10 minutes to heat through thoroughly. Serve in warmed bowls with some ciabatta bread to mop up the juices.

Tomato and Fennel Soup

Serves: 4 *Vegetarian/Vegan*
Preparation time: *20 minutes + 40 minutes cooking*
Freezing: *not recommended*

A versatile soup, delicious in the summer months, which can be served either hot or well chilled depending on the warmth of the day.

1 tablespoon olive oil
1 onion, chopped
1 large bulb fennel, sliced and fronds reserved
1 large carrot, sliced
1 small potato, chopped
700 g (1½ lb) vine-ripened tomatoes, skinned, de-seeded and chopped
700 ml (1¼ pints) vegetable stock (page 14)
sugar to taste
salt
freshly ground black pepper
toasted fennel seeds for garnishing

1 Heat the oil in a large lidded saucepan, add the onion, fennel, carrot and potato, cover and sweat for 20 minutes, shaking the pan occasionally.

2 Add the tomatoes, stock and sugar, bring to the boil, cover and simmer for a further 20 minutes.

3 Cool slightly before liquidising to a purée. Season to taste and serve either hot or really well chilled. Garnish with a few fennel fronds and some toasted fennel seeds if liked.

Tomato Soup with Basil and Olive Pistou

Serves: 4 *Vegetarian*
Preparation time: *20 minutes + 20 minutes cooking*
Freezing: *recommended*

This soup is a stunning contrast of colours – the bright red of the soup and deep green of the pistou. Fresh and pungent, it's evocative of the Mediterranean.

FOR THE PISTOU:
1 clove garlic
½ teaspoon coarse sea salt
75 ml (3 fl oz) extra virgin olive oil
25 g (1 oz) basil leaves
25 g (1 oz) black or green stoned olives
25 g (1 oz) grated Parmesan cheese

FOR THE SOUP:
1 tablespoon olive oil
1 onion, chopped
1 clove garlic, crushed
1 teaspoon red wine vinegar
2 x 400 g (14 oz) cans tomatoes
300 ml (½ pint) vegetable stock (page 14)
1 tablespoon tomato purée
½ teaspoon sugar
salt
freshly ground black pepper

1 The pistou is best made in advance to give the flavours time to develop. In a pestle and mortar cream the garlic and sea salt together to make a paste. Put into a liquidiser with the oil, basil leaves and olives. Process until finely chopped. You will need to keep scraping down the sides with a spatula. Add the Parmesan and pulse until fairly smooth. Cover and set to one side.

2 Heat the oil in a large lidded saucepan. Add the onion and garlic, cover and sweat for 10 minutes.

3 Stir in the vinegar and bubble to evaporate. Add the canned tomatoes, stock, tomato purée and sugar. Bring to the boil, cover and simmer gently for 10 minutes.

4 Allow the soup to cool slightly before liquidising and then pushing through a sieve. Check the seasoning. Return the soup to the rinsed pan and heat through. Divide between warmed serving bowls and spoon a teaspoonful of pistou onto each. Serve at once.

Tip: Pistou is a version of pesto – but without the pine nuts. You will have more than you need to accompany this soup; any left over can be stirred through pasta or used to coat ciabatta and baked for Croûtons (page 48).

Photo: For Pine Nut and Oregano Breadsticks see page 76.

Smokey Aubergine, Chickpea and Mint Soup

Serves: 4 *Vegetarian*
Preparation time: *15 minutes + 45 minutes cooking*
Freezing: *recommended*

Batons of aubergine, dipped in seasoned flour and then fried, make a lovely topping. It's worth making a large enough quantity of soup to warrant using an extra aubergine just for the garnish.

2 large aubergines
1 tablespoon olive oil
1 onion, chopped
2 cloves garlic, crushed
½ teaspoon smoked paprika
400 g can chickpeas, rinsed and drained
600 ml (1 pint) vegetable stock (page 14)
4 tablespoons Greek natural yogurt
2 tablespoons chopped fresh mint
salt
freshly ground black pepper

FOR THE GARNISH:
Greek yogurt
diced cucumber
sprigs of mint

1 Pre-heat the grill to its hottest setting. Prick the aubergines all over with a fork, place them in a roasting tin and grill for about 20 minutes, turning halfway through, until blistered. Plunge the aubergines into a bowl of cold water to cool; they will wizen immediately.

2 Remove the aubergines from the water and pat dry. Slit in half horizontally and, using a spoon, scoop out the flesh. Discard the skins. Chop the flesh into small pieces.

3 While the aubergines are cooling, heat the oil in a large lidded saucepan, add the onion and garlic, cover and sweat for 10 minutes, shaking the pan occasionally.

4 Stir in the paprika and cook for a further minute.

5 Add the aubergines to the pan with the chickpeas and stock. Bring to the boil, cover and simmer for 15 minutes.

6 Cool slightly. Pour half the soup into a blender with the yogurt and mint. Purée to a smooth consistency. Return to the pan with the unpuréed soup and stir to combine.

7 Reheat carefully, without boiling, adjust seasoning to taste and spoon into warmed serving bowls. Garnish with a dollop of yogurt, some cucumber and mint.

Asian Hot and Sour Prawn Soup

Serves: 4
Preparation time: *10 minutes + 25 minutes cooking*
Freezing: *not recommended*

Hot and spicy, sour and salty, this is a very refreshing and very low calorie soup, with a lovely fragrance.

1 litre (1¾ pints) vegetable stock (page 14)
2 stalks lemon grass, bruised
2.5 cm (1 inch) piece fresh ginger, sliced into
    batons
1 red chilli, finely chopped
4 Kaffir lime leaves
1 tablespoon fish sauce
1 tablespoon light soy sauce
1 tablespoon lime juice
1 tablespoon sugar
salt
freshly ground black pepper
225 g (8 oz) oyster mushrooms, stalks
    removed
350 g (12 oz) shelled raw tiger prawns

FOR THE GARNISH:
3–4 spring onions, thinly sliced
handful fresh coriander leaves

1 Pour the stock into a large lidded saucepan. Add the lemon grass, ginger, chilli and lime leaves. Bring to the boil, cover and simmer for 15 minutes to enable the flavours to fuse.

2 Stir in the fish sauce, soy sauce, lime juice and sugar. Check seasoning.

3 Add the mushrooms and simmer for 10 minutes, popping the prawns into the boiling liquor for the final couple of minutes so they turn pink and are just cooked.

4 Ladle into warmed serving bowls, sprinkle the spring onions over the surface and scatter with coriander leaves.

Vichyssoise

Serves: 4
Preparation time: *15 minutes + 30 minutes cooking + chilling time*
Freezing: *recommended before adding cream*

This is one of the simplest and best loved soups. Serve hot in the winter (as leek and potato potage) and chilled under the title of Vichyssoise for the summer months.

1 tablespoon butter
1 onion, chopped
3 leeks, trimmed and sliced
1 medium potato, diced
700 ml (1¼ pints) chicken stock (page 15)
6 tablespoons single cream
salt
freshly ground black pepper
flower ice cubes to garnish

1 Melt the butter in a large lidded saucepan, add the onion, leeks and potato, stir to coat, cover and sweat for 10 minutes, shaking the pan occasionally.

2 Add the chicken stock, bring to the boil, cover and simmer for 20 minutes until the vegetables are tender.

3 Allow to cool slightly before puréeing in a liquidiser. Stir in most of the cream and adjust seasoning.

4 If serving hot, return to the rinsed out pan and re-heat gently without boiling. Spoon into warmed bowls and top with a swirl of cream.

5 For chilled soup, refrigerate for at least a couple of hours (chill the bowls as well). Serve with a swirl of cream and some ice cubes frozen with a single flower in them (such as violet, rosemary or a lavender sprig).

Photo: For Lavender Focaccia see page 75.

Guacamole Gazpacho

Serves: 4
Preparation time: *15 minutes + chilling time*
Freezing: *not recommended*

An easy summer soup with a tangy taste.

4 medium, ripe avocados
juice of 2 limes
600 ml (1 pint) chilled chicken stock (page 15)
    plus extra if needed
1 clove garlic, creamed to a paste with
    ½ teaspoon coarse sea salt
8 spring onions, finely sliced
4 ripe tomatoes, skinned, de-seeded and
    chopped
4 tablespoons chopped fresh coriander
1 fat red chilli, finely chopped
Tabasco
8 ice cubes

1 Remove the stones from the avocados and
   scoop the flesh into a liquidiser with the lime
   juice. Start the motor running and pour in the
   stock in a steady stream. Add a little more
   if necessary to give a smooth, 'spoonable'
   consistency.

2 Add the garlic mixture and pulse briefly to
   blend it in. Pour the soup into a large bowl.

3 Combine the spring onions, tomatoes,
   coriander and chilli and chop them together
   into very small pieces.

4 Keeping just a little aside for a garnish, stir the
   spring onion mixture through the soup. Taste
   and add a few drops of Tabasco if wished.
   Chill for a couple of hours.

5 Just prior to serving put a couple of ice cubes
   in each bowl of soup. When they have melted,
   stir the soup, sprinkle with the reserved onion
   mixture and serve at once.

   Tip: The same rule applies here as to any
   soup that is being served cold – it must be
   very cold. The trick is to dish the soup up
   5 minutes before serving and pop a couple
   of ice cubes into each. Give the soup a
   careful stir just before bringing to the table.

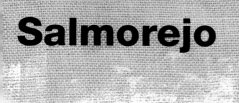

Salmorejo

Serves: 4
Preparation time: *20 minutes + chilling time*
Freezing: *not recommended*

Salmorejo is a speciality of southern Spain, where it is also served as a dip owing to its thickness. Best left overnight to develop its flavour fully, Salmorejo has a distinctive salmon pink colour and is a fabulous soup to make at the height of a hot summer.

900 g (2 lb) vine-ripened tomatoes
1 clove garlic
1 teaspoon coarse sea salt
350 g (12 oz) ciabatta or rustic style day-old
   bread, roughly torn
approximately 125 ml (4 fl oz) cold water
150–175 ml (5–6 fl oz) extra virgin olive oil
2 tablespoons cider or sherry vinegar
salt
freshly ground black pepper

FOR THE GARNISH:
Serrano ham, sliced into strips
1 hard boiled egg white, diced

1 You will need to liquidise this soup in two
   batches.

2 Skin the tomatoes. Scoop out the seeds and
   press them through a sieve to extract the
   juice. Dice the tomato flesh. Put the tomatoes
   and their juices in a liquidiser.

3 Cream the garlic and salt to a purée using a
   pestle and mortar. Add to the liquidiser with
   the bread. Add half the water and run the
   liquidiser, adding enough extra water to
   enable the mixture to blend. This will take
   3–4 minutes of scraping down and pulsing.

4 Drizzle in the oil through the lid of the liquidiser
   and pulse until the soup is very smooth.

5 Add the vinegar, check seasoning and
   refrigerate overnight.

6 Serve garnished with ribbons of ham and
   chopped egg white.

Tip: Salmorejo doesn't require any cooking
and makes use of tomatoes when they are
at their most inexpensive and plentiful. Their
flavour is integral to the success of this
recipe, so make sure that they are ripe and
juicy!

Bouillabaisse

Serves: 4
Preparation time: *20 minutes + 35 minutes cooking*
Freezing: *not recommended*

An extravagant main course soup – delicious on a hot day – served simply with French bread to mop up the juices.

1 tablespoon olive oil
1 small bulb fennel, thinly sliced and fronds
   reserved for garnish
1 small red onion, finely chopped
good pinch saffron strands
1 litre (1¾ pints) hot fish stock (page 16)
225 g (8 oz) tomatoes, peeled, de-seeded and
   diced
1 tablespoon chopped fresh parsley
2 teaspoons chopped fresh dill
2 pieces orange peel, white pith removed
sugar to taste
salt
freshly ground black pepper
700 g (1½ lb) prepared mixed fish (e.g. sole,
   salmon, cod, mussels, prawns, red mullet,
   bass, monkfish) cut into largish pieces

1 Heat the oil in a large lidded saucepan, add the fennel and onion, cover and sweat for 15 minutes, shaking the pan occasionally.

2 Meanwhile, soak the saffron strands in the hot stock.

3 Add the stock and saffron to the pan with the tomatoes, their juices, the herbs, orange peel and sugar. Bring to the boil, cover and simmer for 15 minutes.

4 Remove the orange peel. Taste the soup and season if necessary. Stir in the fish, adding the thicker cuts to start with. Bear in mind that they will continue to cook in the liquor after removing from the heat – so they should take between 2–4 minutes to cook. Shellfish will only take a minute or two to heat through.

5 Ladle into warmed serving bowls, scatter with some fennel fronds and serve at once.

Tip: Prepare the base (up to the end of step 3) ahead of time. Re-heat and add the fish just prior to serving.

Summer Chicken Soup

Serves: 4
Preparation time: *15 minutes + 20 minutes cooking*
Freezing: *not recommended*

This is a soup for one of those rainy days when summer seems to have disappeared behind a cloud!

½ tablespoon oil
115 g (4 oz) shallots, roughly chopped
175 g (6 oz) chicken thighs, diced
450 g (1 lb) tomatoes, skinned, de-seeded and diced
1 good-sized courgette, grated
1 tablespoon chopped fresh oregano
1 tablespoon chopped fresh basil
1 tablespoon chopped fresh parsley
700 ml (1¼ pints) chicken stock (page 15)
sugar to taste
salt
freshly ground black pepper

1 Heat the oil in a large lidded saucepan; add the shallots and chicken and fry for 2–3 minutes, stirring continuously, until golden.

2 Add the tomatoes, courgette, herbs, stock and a little sugar. Bring to the boil, cover and simmer gently for 15 minutes.

3 Season to taste and serve in warmed bowls.

Salmon and Prawn Summer Soup

Serves: 6
Preparation time: *20 minutes + 30 minutes cooking*
Freezing: *not recommended*

This is a lovely soup to serve in the summer months. The light base belies the richness of the salmon, and chopped tomatoes provide a subtly flavoured background. Potato and Rosemary Bread (page 139) or Pine Nut and Oregano Bread Sticks (page 76) would both go equally well with this.

15 g (½ oz) butter
2 trimmed leeks, thinly sliced
700 g (1½ lb) tomatoes, skinned, de-seeded
  and chopped
2 medium potatoes, diced
1.2 litres (2 pints) fish stock (page 16)
good pinch sugar
bay leaf
350 g (12 oz) salmon fillet, skinned and cut
  into bite size cubes
175 g (6 oz) cooked and peeled prawns
4 tablespoons mascarpone
3 tablespoons chopped fresh basil
salt
freshly ground black pepper

1 Melt the butter in a large lidded saucepan. Add the leeks, cover and sweat for 5 minutes until soft.

2 Add the tomatoes, potatoes, stock, sugar and bay leaf, bring to the boil, cover and simmer for 20 minutes.

3 Stir in the salmon and bubble gently for 3 minutes. Add the prawns and heat through for 1–2 minutes.

4 Add the mascarpone and basil. Season to taste. Ensure that the soup is heated through before serving.

Watercress and Orange Soup

Serves: 4 *Vegetarian*
Preparation time: *15 minutes + 15 minutes cooking*
Freezing: *not recommended*

This refreshing soup is equally good hot or cold.

1 tablespoon olive oil
1 medium onion, chopped
1 medium potato, chopped
rind of ½ orange
juice of 1 orange
2 x 80 g bags of watercress
850 ml (1½ pints) vegetable stock (page 14)
2 teaspoons soft brown sugar
salt
freshly ground black pepper
4 tablespoons double cream
2 tablespoons roughly chopped toasted
    hazelnuts

1 Heat the oil in a large lidded saucepan, add the onion and potato, stir to coat, cover and sweat for 10 minutes, shaking the pan occasionally, until the onion has softened.

2 Meanwhile, pare thin strips from half the orange. Place in a cup and pour boiling water over. Strain after 30 seconds and plunge into cold water. Put to one side.

3 Add the orange juice, watercress (reserving four sprigs for garnish), stock and sugar to the soup. Simmer for 5 minutes, just to wilt the watercress.

4 Cool slightly, then purée in a liquidiser until smooth and adjust seasoning. If serving cold, refrigerate.

5 To finish, divide the soup between four serving bowls, swirl a tablespoon of cream over each portion, arrange the strips of orange rind on top and scatter the chopped nuts over.

Lavender Focaccia

Serves: 8 *Vegetarian/Vegan*
Preparation time: *20 minutes + 80 minutes proving + 15–20 minutes cooking*
Freezing: *recommended*

A beautiful fragrant bread for summer days – present at the table decorated with some sprigs of lavender, and serve in strips or wedges.

350 g (12 oz) strong white bread flour
1 sachet easy blend yeast
½ teaspoon coarse sea salt, plus extra for
   sprinkling
200 ml (7 fl oz) warm water
3 tablespoons olive oil, plus extra for brushing
4 heads lavender, crumbled

1 Place the flour, yeast and salt in a bowl. Add the water and oil and mix to a soft dough.

2 Turn out onto work surface and knead for about 10 minutes until smooth. Place in an oiled polythene bag and leave in a warm place to prove for about 1 hour.

3 Pre-heat the oven to Gas Mark 7/ 220°C/425°F. Grease a baking sheet.

4 On a lightly floured surface, roll out the dough to 1 cm (½ inch) thick. Transfer onto the baking sheet, cover and prove for a further 20 minutes.

5 Using your finger tips, make deep indentations in the surface of the dough. Brush with oil and scatter with the lavender flower heads. Finish with a light sprinkling of sea salt.

6 Bake in the centre of the oven for 15–20 minutes. Transfer to a wire rack to cool.

Illustrated on page 67.

Pine Nut and Oregano Breadsticks

Makes: 24 *Vegetarian*
Preparation time: *25 minutes + 70 minutes proving + 15 minutes baking*
Freezing: *recommended*

Breadsticks or grissini make a particularly good accompaniment to tomato-based soups.

350 g (12 oz) strong white bread flour
1 sachet easy blend yeast
1 tablespoon toasted pine nuts
¾ teaspoon dried oregano
½ teaspoon coarse sea salt, plus extra for sprinkling
2 tablespoons olive oil, plus extra for brushing
200 ml (7fl oz) warm milk

1 Place the flour, yeast, pine nuts, oregano and salt in a bowl. Stir to combine.

2 Add the oil and milk, mix to a soft dough, then turn out onto work surface and knead for 10 minutes until smooth.

3 Place the dough in an oiled polythene bag and leave in a warm place to prove until doubled in size – about 1 hour.

4 Pre-heat the oven to Gas Mark 5/ 190°C/375°F. Grease two baking sheets.

5 Divide the dough into 24 pieces and roll each out, on an unfloured work surface, into 23 cm (9 inch) lengths. This is easiest if you don't knock the dough back first. Using your fingers, work from the middle outwards, pressing down quite firmly, and splaying your fingers as you work towards the ends.

6 Arrange the breadsticks on the baking sheets, ensuring that they are not touching. Brush with olive oil and sprinkle with sea salt.

7 Cover again to stop them drying out, and allow to prove for 10 minutes.

8 Bake in the middle of the oven for about 15 minutes, until golden. Cool on a wire rack.

Tip: Try varying these by adding Parmesan, hazelnuts and poppy or sesame seeds.

Illustrated on page 63.

Feta, Olive and Tomato Scones

Makes: 10–12 *Vegetarian*
Preparation time: *15 minutes + 10–12 minutes baking*
Freezing: *recommended*

These make a tasty accompaniment to any tomato-based soup.

225 g (8 oz) self-raising flour
1 teaspoon baking powder
1 teaspoon dried oregano
good pinch cayenne pepper
80 g (3 oz) butter
80 g (3 oz) Feta cheese, diced small
25 g (1 oz) grated Parmesan cheese
25 g (1 oz) black or green olives, stoned and
   chopped
6 halves sun-dried tomatoes in oil, snipped
150 ml (¼ pint) milk soured with 1 teaspoon
   lemon juice
milk for brushing

1 Pre-heat the oven to Gas Mark 8/ 230°C/450°F. Lightly grease a baking tray.

2 Mix together the flour, baking powder, oregano and cayenne pepper in a bowl. Rub in the butter.

3 Crumble in the Feta and stir in the Parmesan, olives and sun-dried tomatoes.

4 Add enough milk to the dry ingredients to make them stick together. Turn out onto a lightly floured surface and knead just enough to form a soft dough.

5 Roll the dough out into an oblong measuring 20 x 15 cm (8 x 6 inches). Using a sharp knife, cut into 8–10 rectangles. Space them well apart on the baking tray. Brush with milk and bake for 10–12 minutes, until risen and golden.

6 Transfer to a wire rack to cool slightly. Best served warm.

Pistachio and Pecorino Biscotti

Makes: 12 *Vegetarian*
Preparation time: *15 minutes + 40–45 minutes baking*
Freezing: *not recommended*

These nutty biscuits are similar to mini crisp breads and best served with cold soups.

80 g (3 oz) plain flour
½ teaspoon baking powder
40 g (1½ oz) shelled pistachio nuts
25 g (1 oz) grated Parmesan cheese
good pinch salt
plenty of freshly ground black pepper
1 egg, beaten
approximately 1 tablespoon milk

1 Pre-heat the oven to Gas Mark 4/
180°C/350°F. Lightly grease a baking sheet.

2 In a small mixing bowl combine the flour,
baking powder, pistachio nuts, Parmesan and
seasoning.

3 Make a well in the centre of the dry mixture
and add the egg and enough milk to make a
soft dough.

4 Turn out onto a lightly floured work surface
and shape into an oblong about 4.5 cm
(1¾ inch) in diameter. Place on the baking
sheet and flatten slightly to measure roughly
7 cm (2¾ inches) across. Cook in the centre
of the oven for 25 minutes.

5 Using a serrated or bread knife, slice the
oblong diagonally into 1 cm- (½ inch-) thick
slices. Lay these flat down on the baking
sheet and return them to oven for another
15–20 minutes, until golden and crisp.

6 Cool on a wire rack before serving. The
biscotti store well in an airtight container for
3–4 days.

Tips: These biscotti are versatile in that
they also double up as croustades, perfect
for finishing with various toppings as
canapés.

Almonds and Brazil nuts also work well in
this recipe and would need to be roughly
chopped before adding.

Rocket Frittata

Serves: 8 *Vegetarian*
Preparation time: *10 minutes + 20–25 minutes cooking*
Freezing: *not recommended*

These omelettes, eaten cold, are very popular in Italy and Spain. They make an interesting alternative to bread. Potato-based, add any vegetables that you like to complement the soup you are serving.

350 g (12 oz) new potatoes, very thinly sliced
2 tablespoons olive oil
6 eggs
25 g (1oz) grated Parmesan cheese
1½ tablespoons chives, snipped
freshly ground black pepper
25 g (1 oz) rocket

1 Rinse the potatoes in cold water to remove some of the starch. Pat dry between two tea towels.

2 Heat the oil in a 25 cm (10 inch) non-stick frying pan with a heat-proof handle. Add the potatoes and fry gently for about 15 minutes until cooked and just colouring. Stir them around in the pan, turning them over occasionally.

3 Pre-heat the grill to a medium/high temperature.

4 Lightly beat together the eggs, Parmesan and chives. Season with pepper (the Parmesan means that you probably won't need any salt).

5 Scatter the rocket over the potatoes and then pour the egg mixture over the top. Cook gently for 3 minutes to set the underneath, shaking the pan occasionally but not stirring. Press the rocket down if it rises to the top.

6 Now place the frying pan under the grill and cook for a further 3–4 minutes until puffy and golden and the egg is set.

7 Allow to cool in the pan and serve, sliced into wedges, at room temperature or cold from the fridge.

Autumn

Autumn days bring with them a scramble for the last of the ripened sweetcorn, swollen aubergines, sweet bell peppers, pumpkins and squashes. What better means of stretching their presence into the oncoming months than preserving them in the form of soups, ready to be resurrected on colder days. A trigger to rekindle fond memories of seasons passed.

Cauliflower Soup with Roasted Cashew Nuts

Serves: 4 *Vegetarian*
Preparation time: *15 minutes + 35 minutes cooking*
Freezing: *recommended*

A cheesy flavoured soup with a lovely consistency.

25 g (1 oz) butter
80 g (3 oz) cashew nuts, roughly chopped
1 onion, chopped
1 clove garlic, crushed
1 medium potato, diced
1 medium cauliflower, divided into florets
850 ml (1½ pints) vegetable stock (page 14)
115 g (4 oz) Cheddar cheese, grated
salt
freshly ground black pepper

FOR THE GARNISH:
15 g (½ oz) butter
50 g (2 oz) whole cashew nuts

1 Melt the butter in a large lidded saucepan and brown the chopped cashew nuts for about a minute.

2 Stir in the onion, garlic and potato, cover and sweat for 10 minutes, shaking the pan occasionally.

3 Add the cauliflower and stock, bring to the boil, cover and simmer for 20 minutes, or until the cauliflower is tender.

4 Remove from the heat and blend in the cheese. Allow to cool slightly.

5 Blend a scant half of the mixture and then stir this through the rest of the soup so that you can actually see pieces of cauliflower and nut.

6 Re-heat very gently without boiling, so as not to toughen the cheese. Check seasoning.

7 Meanwhile, fry the whole nuts for a couple of minutes in the butter until golden. Drain on kitchen paper.

8 Ladle the soup into warmed serving bowls and scatter the nuts over the top.

Tips: Adding 50 g (2 oz) sliced chorizo when cooking the onion gives an even fuller flavoured soup.

If you prefer your soup with a more even consistency, purée it all rather than just half.

Haddock and Mash Soup

Serves: 4
Preparation time: *10 minutes + 25 minutes cooking*
Freezing: *not recommended*

This is a very useful soup to have 'up your sleeve' – quick and easy to make it really delivers on flavour – and uses very few ingredients.

25 g (1 oz) butter
1 onion, chopped fairly finely
450 g (1 lb) potatoes, diced
good pinch medium curry powder
350 g (12 oz) undyed smoked haddock fillet,
    skinned
300 ml (½ pint) milk
300 ml (½ pint) water
freshly ground black pepper
4 tablespoons double cream
2 tablespoons chopped fresh parsley

1 Melt the butter in a large lidded saucepan, add the onion, potatoes and curry powder, cover and sweat for 10 minutes, shaking the pan occasionally.

2 Lay the haddock over the vegetables and pour in the milk and water. Season with plenty of black pepper. Bring to the boil, cover and simmer for 10–12 minutes, until the potatoes are soft and the fish is creamy.

3 Remove from the heat. Using a potato masher, crush the fish and potatoes to give an even but still fairly rough consistency.

4 Stir in the cream and parsley, re-heat gently if necessary and serve.

Fondue Style Onion Soup

Serves: 6
Preparation time: *15 minutes + 55 minutes cooking*
Freezing: *not recommended*

Perhaps this should have been titled 'Swiss Onion Soup'. If you have the time, simmer for longer than the 30 minutes recommended here to break the onion down even further.

50 g (2 oz) butter
900 g (2 lb) onions, thinly sliced (a food
   processor is excellent for this)
2 cloves garlic, crushed
1 teaspoon sugar
850 ml (1½ pints) chicken stock (page 15)
425 ml (¾ pint) dry white wine
175 g (6 oz) Gruyère cheese, grated
2 tablespoons corn flour
2 tablespoons Kirsch, vermouth or water
grated nutmeg
salt
freshly ground black pepper

TO SERVE:
rustic Croûtons (page 48)
grated Gruyère cheese

1 Melt the butter in a large lidded pan (a casserole dish is good for this recipe). Stir in the onions, garlic and sugar, and toss to coat. Fry over a medium heat for 20 minutes until rich, golden brown and softened.

2 Pour in the chicken stock and wine, bring to the boil, cover and simmer gently for at least 30 minutes.

3 Gradually stir in the Gruyère over a low heat.

4 Blend the corn flour to a smooth paste with the Kirsch, vermouth, or water if you prefer. Spoon a ladle from the soup onto the corn flour and stir in. Return it to the pan and keep stirring until the soup thickens.

5 Season with nutmeg, salt and pepper. This dish is good served from a large tureen in the centre of the table so that everyone helps themselves. Hand round bowls of Croûtons for a crisp contrast and extra grated Gruyère to melt into the soup.

Tip: Rarebit Croustades (page 108) would make a good alternative accompaniment here.

Fennel, Pear and Red Pepper Soup

Serves: 4–6
Preparation time: *20 minutes + 40 minutes cooking*
Freezing: *not recommended*

A lovely soup full of autumn flavours.

1 tablespoon olive oil
1 onion, chopped
1 bulb fennel, thinly sliced
2 red peppers, de-seeded
1 large carrot, sliced
2 juicy pears, peeled, cored and thinly sliced
3 tablespoons basil leaves
850 ml (1½ pints) chicken stock (page 15)
sugar
4 tablespoons Greek natural yogurt
salt
freshly ground black pepper

FOR THE GARNISH:
4 teaspoons Greek natural yogurt
½ pear, peeled, cored and thinly sliced
basil leaves

1 Heat the oil in a large lidded saucepan; add the onion, fennel, peppers and carrot. Cover and sweat for 20 minutes, shaking the pan occasionally.

2 Add the pears, basil, stock and sugar. Bring to the boil, cover and simmer for 20 minutes.

3 Cool slightly before liquidising until smooth and then pushing through a sieve.

4 Return to the rinsed out pan, stir in the yogurt and test seasoning. Re-heat gently before dividing between warmed serving bowls and garnishing with yogurt, the sliced pear and basil leaves.

Courgette Soup with Golden Shallots

Serves: 4
Preparation time: *15 minutes + 25 minutes cooking*
Freezing: *not recommended*

Any gardener will tell you that when courgettes are in season it is hard to keep pace in terms of consumption. This soup is a great way to make use of some of the glut.

175 g (6 oz or approximately 12) shallots
25 g (1 oz) butter
700 g (1½ lb) courgettes, sliced
300 ml (½ pint) chicken stock (page 15)
150 ml (¼ pint) white wine
1 teaspoon sugar
2 teaspoons chopped fresh oregano
salt
freshly ground black pepper

FOR THE GARNISH:
1 tablespoon olive oil
50 g (2 oz) shallots, thinly sliced into rings
sprigs golden oregano

1 To peel the shallots, place them in a bowl, cover with boiling water and strain after 1 minute. The skins will peel off easily when cool enough to handle. Chop them roughly.

2 Melt the butter in a large lidded saucepan; add the shallots and courgette and sweat for 10 minutes.

3 Add the stock, white wine, sugar and oregano, bring to the boil, cover and simmer for 10 minutes. Cool slightly before puréeing in a liquidiser.

4 For the garnish, heat the oil and fry the shallots for about 3 minutes until golden. Drain on kitchen paper.

5 Re-heat the soup and check seasoning. Serve in warmed bowls with rings of shallots and sprigs of oregano.

Sweet Pepper and Chorizo Soup

Serves: 4
Preparation time: *15 minutes + 55 minutes cooking*
Freezing: *recommended*

Chorizo gives this soup a lovely rounded flavour and helps achieve its wonderful bright colour.

4 red peppers
1 tablespoon olive oil
50 g (2 oz) chorizo slices, snipped
1 onion, chopped
1 clove garlic, crushed
1 tablespoon tomato purée
600 ml (1 pint) chicken stock (page 15)
1 tablespoon chopped fresh oregano leaves
sugar to taste
salt
freshly ground black pepper

FOR THE GARNISH:
4 slices chorizo, lightly fried on each side
sprigs of basil or oregano

1 Heat the oven to Gas Mark 6/200°C/400°F. Place the peppers, just as they are, in a roasting tin and bake them for 25–30 minutes until charred and soft.

2 Remove the peppers from the oven and carefully transfer them to a polythene bag. Seal and leave them to cool until cold enough to handle. When cool, peel the skins away and remove the seeds. Save the precious juices to add to the soup with the stock. Roughly chop the flesh.

3 Heat the oil in a large lidded saucepan and add the chorizo, onion and garlic. Fry until golden and the onion has softened, about 4–5 minutes.

4 Add the chopped peppers and stir for 1 minute.

5 Blend in the tomato purée, stock, oregano and sugar. Bring to the boil, cover and simmer for 20 minutes.

6 Cool the soup slightly before liquidising to a purée. Return to the rinsed out pan and re-heat gently. Adjust seasoning.

7 Ladle the soup into warmed bowls, float a chorizo slice on each serving and garnish with basil or oregano.

Photo: For Bruschetta with Tapenade see page 105.

Chicken Noodle Soup with Sesame Dumplings

Serves: 4
Preparation time: *10 minutes + 12 minutes cooking*
Freezing: *not recommended*

This is a real comfort soup, especially if you include the sesame Dumplings (page 106). Remember to toast the sesame seeds first for maximum flavour and to use a really good chicken stock.

1.4 litres (2½ pints) chicken stock (page 15)
1 large carrot, thinly sliced
115 g (4 oz) dried fine egg noodles
175 g (6 oz) cooked chicken, shredded
198 g can sweet corn, drained
115 g (4 oz) frozen peas
2 tablespoons chopped fresh parsley
sesame Dumplings (page 106, optional)
salt
freshly ground black pepper

1 Bring the stock to the boil in a large lidded saucepan and make sure that you have all your ingredients prepared.

2 Add the carrot to the pan and simmer for 2 minutes.

3 Stir in the noodles, chicken, sweet corn, peas and parsley. Bring to the boil and place the dumplings, if using, on top. Cover and simmer for 10 minutes.

4 Season to taste and serve at once.

Tip: Flower-shaped carrot slices – made by drawing a canelle knife down the carrot's length before slicing – make this soup look especially pretty.

Carrot and Apple Soup

Serves: 6 *Vegetarian*
Preparation time: *15 minutes + 40 minutes cooking*
Freezing: *recommended*

The crunchy garnish to accompany this soup needs to be made no more than an hour before serving.

1 tablespoon butter
1 onion, chopped
450 g (1 lb) carrots, chopped
175 g (6 oz) parsnips, chopped
1.2 litres (2 pints) vegetable stock (page 14)
2 medium Bramley apples, chopped
2 teaspoons soft brown sugar
salt
freshly ground black pepper

FOR THE GARNISH:
½ green eating apple
2 centre stalks celery with leaves
1 tablespoon chopped fresh parsley
2 teaspoons cider vinegar

1 Melt the butter in a large lidded saucepan, add the onion, carrots and parsnips, cover and sweat for 10 minutes, shaking the pan occasionally.

2 Add the stock, apples and sugar, bring to the boil, cover and simmer for 30 minutes. Allow to cool slightly before liquidising until smooth. Adjust seasoning.

3 For the garnish, dice the apple and celery very finely. Mix with the parsley and vinegar.

4 Return the soup to the rinsed out pan and re-heat. Divide between warmed serving bowls and spoon some crunchy apple garnish onto each.

Beetroot and Ginger Soup with Feta

Serves: 4 *Vegetarian*
Preparation time: *15 minutes + 45 minutes roasting*
Freezing: *recommended*

This is not a shy soup – it has the most amazing colour and bold flavour, the sweetness of which is dramatically offset by the tangy sharpness of crumbled Feta cheese. Having a cold soup as an autumn standby is useful during those frequent Indian Summers we seem to have nowadays.

700 g (1½ lb) uncooked beetroot, peeled and
  cut into wedges
1 onion, cut into wedges
2 medium carrots, sliced thickly
3 tablespoons olive oil
salt
freshly ground black pepper
4 tablespoons syrup from a jar of stem ginger
850 ml (1½ pints) vegetable stock (page 14)
4 tablespoons Greek yogurt

FOR THE GARNISH:
Feta cheese, crumbled
toasted pine nuts
sprigs of mint

1 Heat the oven to Gas Mark 6/200°C/400°F.

2 Place the vegetables in a large roasting pan, drizzle with the oil and mix well to coat. Season.

3 Roast towards the top of the oven for 45 minutes. Turn the vegetables half way through cooking.

4 About 10 minutes before the end of roasting spoon the ginger syrup over the vegetables. Return them to the oven.

5 Remove the vegetables from the oven, cool slightly and liquidise in batches with most of the stock.

6 Pour the remaining stock into the roasting pan and scrape off any charred bits of beetroot. Add this all to the soup with the yogurt and blitz for a few seconds.

7 Chill the soup well. Serve in ice-cold bowls with a little Feta cheese crumbled onto the centre, a sprinkling of pine nuts and a sprig of mint.

Aubergine, Almond and Apricot Soup

Serves: *Vegetarian*
Preparation time: *15 minutes + 50–55 minutes cooking*
Freezing: *recommended*

These ingredients have a sublime affinity, and the toasted almonds give a delicious undercurrent to the soup.

2 medium aubergines, thinly sliced
olive oil for brushing
salt
freshly ground black pepper
1 tablespoon olive oil
1 onion, chopped
1 clove garlic, crushed
2 teaspoons grated gresh ginger
2 teaspoons ground coriander
1 teaspoon cumin seeds
¼ teaspoon turmeric
1.2 litres (2 pints) vegetable stock (page 14)
115 g (4 oz) dried apricots, roughly chopped
4 tablespoons Marsala or sherry
2 tablespoons clear honey
squeeze lemon juice
80 g (3 oz) lightly toasted ground almonds

FOR THE GARNISH:
4 teaspoons Greek natural yogurt
sprigs of mint

1 Heat the grill to fairly high. Spread the aubergines out on a rack over a grill pan. Brush lightly with oil and season. Grill on both sides for about 12–20 minutes until golden.

2 Meanwhile, heat the oil in a large lidded saucepan. Add the onion, garlic, ginger, coriander, cumin seeds and turmeric. Cover and sweat for 10 minutes.

3 Stir the grilled aubergines into the onion mixture with the stock, apricots, Marsala, honey and lemon juice. Bring to the boil, cover and simmer for 20 minutes.

4 Add the almonds and simmer for 5 minutes.

5 Allow to cool slightly before puréeing until smooth. Check seasoning.

6 Return to the rinsed out pan and re-heat slowly. Divide between warmed serving bowls and top with yogurt and a sprig of mint.

Pumpkin, Beef and Chilli Soup

Serves: 4
Preparation time: *15 minutes + 35 minutes cooking*
Freezing: *recommended*

A warming soup for those cooler autumn days.

2 tablespoons olive oil

1 onion, chopped

1 green chilli, de-seeded and finely chopped

1 clove garlic, crushed

450 g (1 lb) pumpkin flesh, diced

1 large carrot, diced

225 g (8 oz) rump steak, cut into bite-sized
chunks

½ teaspoon turmeric

1.2 litres (2 pints) vegetable stock (page 14)

410 g can green lentils, rinsed and drained

2 tablespoons chopped rosemary

2 tablespoons chopped fresh parsley

2 teaspoons grated fresh ginger

salt

freshly ground black pepper

1 Heat the oil in a large lidded saucepan, add
the onion, chilli, garlic, pumpkin and carrot,
cover and sweat for 10 minutes, shaking the
pan occasionally.

2 Turn up the heat slightly and add the steak
and turmeric. Stir them around for about
1 minute to brown the meat.

3 Add the stock, lentils, herbs and ginger. Bring
to the boil, cover and simmer for 25 minutes.

4 Taste for seasoning before ladling into warmed
bowls to serve.

Roasted Root Vegetable Soup

Serves: **4–6** *Vegetarian/Vegan*
Preparation time: *20 minutes + 40 minutes cooking*
Freezing: *recommended*

Truly a soup you can stand up your spoon in – this is a kitchen table, not a dining table, soup! A thick autumn vegetable purée that requires very little attention and gives a satisfying result.

½ medium celeriac, thickly peeled and cut into
   chunks
½ medium swede, thickly peeled and cut into
   chunks
1 medium parsnip, thickly peeled and cut into
   chunks
2 carrots, cut into chunks
1 large onion, peeled and cut into wedges
½ bulb of garlic, separated and white papery
   skin only removed
2 tablespoons olive oil
1 tablespoon balsamic vinegar
2 sprigs rosemary
salt
freshly ground black pepper
700 ml (1¼ pints) vegetable stock (page 14)
chopped fresh parsley to garnish

1 Pre-heat the oven to Gas Mark 6/
   200°C/400°F.

2 Place all the vegetables and garlic in a
   roasting pan.

3 Drizzle the olive oil and vinegar over, and scatter with the whole rosemary sprigs. Season with salt and pepper and then combine everything thoroughly (I find a couple of large spoons or slotted slices good for this).

4 Cook on the highest oven shelf for 30–40 minutes, turning once half way through, until the vegetables are cooked and slightly charred at the edges.

5 Remove from the oven and discard the rosemary. Try to find all the garlic cloves and, using a sharp knife, split open their skins and scrape out the creamy paste inside.

6 Liquidise the vegetables with their juices, garlic and the stock in batches until smooth.

7 Re-heat gently and serve sprinkled with parsley.

Tip: The suggested vegetables are just a guide; substitute them with whatever is in its prime.

Tuscan Bean Soup

Serves: 4 generous helpings!
Preparation time: *10 minutes + 55 minutes cooking*
Freezing: *recommended*

Packed with a mixture of beans, loads of garlic, pancetta, tomato and herbs, this is a soup truly evocative of Italian provincial cooking.

1 tablespoon olive oil

8 slices smoked pancetta, snipped into pieces

2 onions, finely chopped

4 cloves garlic, crushed

900 g (2 lb) tomatoes, skinned, de-seeded and chopped

2 x 410 g cans mixed beans, rinsed and drained

1.2 litres (2 pints) vegetable stock (page 14)

4 tablespoons chopped fresh parsley

2 sprigs thyme

1 bay leaf

2 teaspoons sugar

salt

freshly ground black pepper

1 Heat the oil in a large lidded saucepan, add the pancetta and fry over a medium heat for 2–3 minutes, until crisp and golden.

2 Add the onions and garlic and cook, turning occasionally, for about 8 minutes, until the onions are tinged brown at the edges.

3 Stir in the tomatoes, beans, stock, herbs and sugar. Bring to the boil, cover and simmer for 45 minutes.

4 Taste, and adjust seasoning if necessary. Serve in warmed bowls.

Tip: Olive and sun-dried tomato Grissini Pastry Puffs (page 107) would make a good accompaniment.

Spiced Lamb Soup

Serves: 6
Preparation time: *10 minutes + 40 minutes cooking*
Freezing: *recommended*

Tender lamb in a warming soup flavoured with ginger and cinnamon; cannellini beans add substance to make this a meal on its own.

1 tablespoon olive oil

1 onion, sliced

1 clove garlic, crushed

2 teaspoons freshly grated ginger

2 teaspoons ground coriander

1 teaspoon ground cumin

1 stick cinnamon

350 g (12 oz) neck of lamb fillet, cut into small
    pieces

410 g can cannellini beans, rinsed and drained

600 ml (1 pint) lamb stock (page 17)

600 ml (1 pint) passatta

2 tablespoons tomato purée

squeeze lemon juice

large sprig rosemary

bay leaf

sugar to taste

salt

freshly ground black pepper

sprigs of rosemary to garnish

1 Heat the oil in a large lidded saucepan. Add the onion, garlic and spices. Fry, uncovered, over a fairly high heat, stirring occasionally, for about 10 minutes or until the onion is golden.

2 Add the lamb and stir round briskly for 1–2 minutes to brown.

3 Stir in the beans, stock, passatta, tomato purée, lemon juice, rosemary, bay leaf and sugar. Bring to the boil, cover and simmer gently for 25–30 minutes.

4 Remove the cinnamon stick, rosemary and bay leaf. Adjust seasoning to taste and serve, garnished with sprigs of rosemary.

Curried Kumara (Sweet Potato) Soup

Serves: 4 *Vegetarian*
Preparation time: *15 minutes + 30 minutes cooking*
Freezing: *recommended*

I was introduced to this beautiful Maori sweet potato by a New Zealand member of the family. Kumara has the most lovely magenta-coloured skin and white flesh flecked with a gorgeous reddish/purple colour, which sadly discolours on cooking.

1 tablespoon butter
1 tablespoon olive oil
450 g (1 lb) kumara, or sweet potato, peeled, quartered and sliced
1 medium onion, chopped
1 teaspoon medium curry powder
700 ml (1¼ pints) vegetable stock (page 14)
15 g (½ oz) coriander
40 g (1½ oz) creamed coconut, thinly sliced
salt
freshly ground black pepper

1 Heat the butter and oil in a large lidded saucepan. Add the kumara and onion and stir in the curry powder to coat. Cover and sweat for 10 minutes, shaking the pan occasionally.

2 Add in the stock and stalks only of the coriander. Bring to the boil, cover and simmer for 20 minutes.

3 Remove from the heat. Roughly chop the coriander leaves and stir most of them into the soup with the creamed coconut. Cool slightly before puréeing until smooth.

4 Re-heat the soup gently. Adjust seasoning and serve in warmed bowls sprinkled with the reserved coriander leaves.

Tip: If you prefer, substitute the curry powder for 1 tablespoon korma curry paste.

Wild Mushroom Soup with Green Herb Butter

Serves: 4 *Vegetarian*
Preparation time: *20 minutes soaking + 5 minutes + 40 minutes cooking*
Freezing: *recommended*

This is an 'earthy' soup with a strong flavour. The herb butter provides an interesting contrast and another taste dimension.

25 g (1 oz) dried porcini mushrooms
425 ml (¾ pint) warm water
25 g (1 oz) butter
1 onion, chopped
1 clove garlic, crushed
225 g (8 oz) chestnut mushrooms, sliced
1 tablespoon flour
600 ml (1 pint) vegetable stock (page 14)
salt
freshly ground black pepper

FOR THE GREEN HERB BUTTER:
50 g (2 oz) softened butter
2 tablespoons chopped fresh parsley
2 teaspoons chopped tarragon
lemon juice
salt
freshly ground black pepper

1 Put the porcini in a small bowl and cover with the warm water. Leave to soak for 30 minutes. Strain through a sieve into a bowl, pushing out most of the moisture with the back of a spoon. Reserve the liquor.

2 Melt the butter in a large lidded saucepan. Add the onion and garlic, cover and sweat for 10 minutes, shaking the pan occasionally.

3 Add the sliced chestnut mushrooms and stir around for 2–3 minutes.

4 Stir in the flour and cook for a couple more minutes.

5 Gradually blend in the stock and reserved mushroom liquor. Bring to the boil, cover and simmer for 25 minutes.

6 Allow to cool slightly before puréeing in a liquidiser. Adjust seasoning and heat through gently.

7 For the herb butter, beat together all the ingredients and adjust lemon juice and seasoning to taste.

8 Divide the soup between warmed bowls. Divide butter into four. Shape each piece between two teaspoons into an oblong. Slide into each bowl of mushroom soup and let your guests stir it through at the table.

Bruschetta with Tapenade

Makes: 8 toasts *Vegetarian*
Preparation time: *10 minutes + 15 minutes cooking*
Freezing: *not recommended*

This tapenade is incredibly easy to make and understandably tastes much fresher than any shop-bought variety. Traditionally, anchovies are included in the recipe, but I think it works equally well without, like this. Do bear in mind that tapenade has a very strong flavour, so be careful which soups you choose to partner it with. Italian tomato or bean-based soups are able to take it!

125 g (4½ oz) black olives, stoned
2 tablespoons capers, drained
1 small clove garlic
2 tablespoons chopped fresh parsley
4 teaspoons extra virgin olive oil
1 teaspoon lemon juice
½ teaspoon dried oregano

FOR THE BRUSCHETTA:
Approximately ¼ stick day-old French loaf or ciabatta bread
A little olive oil for brushing

1 Finely chop the olives, capers and garlic until almost minced. Stir in the remaining ingredients and leave to stand for 1 hour to allow the flavours to mingle.

3 Pre-heat the oven to Gas Mark 4/ 180°C/350°F.

4 Slice the bread into eight 15 mm- (⅝ inch-) thick pieces. Brush one side lightly with oil and place face down on a baking sheet. Cook in the middle of the oven for 15 minutes until crisp. Cool on a wire rack.

5 When ready to serve, spoon the tapenade onto the bruschetta and press down lightly or spread, depending on the texture.

Tips: Try using green olives if you prefer or, to subtly change the flavour, ones that have been marinated in chilli.

Bake the bread a maximum of 1 hour before serving; otherwise it tends to go soggy. As an alternative you could buy thin crispbreads.

As an alternative method, chop the olives, capers and garlic with the oil in a liquidiser, making sure that you leave some texture. Whizz in the parsley, lemon juice and oregano.

Illustrated on page 91.

Dumplings

Makes: 8, serves 4
Preparation time: *5 minutes + 10 minutes cooking*
Freezing: *not recommended*

These are wonderful for turning a soup into a meal. Their name always strikes me as an incredibly inappropriate description for a food that should turn out more akin to a fluffy cloud than a heavy, sodden lump! Dumplings are usually served on top of soup that has not been puréed. They are extremely quick and easy to make; simply pop them into the pan 10 minutes before the end of cooking and they'll take care of themselves! Crème fraîche gives them a delicious flavour, and the suet ensures that they remain light.

FOR THE DOUGH:
50 g (2 oz) self-raising flour
25 g (1 oz) suet
pinch salt
2 tablespoons crème fraîche
a little water

FOR HERBY DUMPLINGS:
1 teaspoon chopped fresh herbs (parsley, thyme, tarragon or sage)

FOR SEEDED DUMPLINGS:
1 teaspoon toasted sesame, fennel or caraway seeds

1 Mix the flour, suet and salt together in a small bowl. Add herbs or seeds if using.

2 Stir in the crème fraîche and sprinkle over enough water (about 1 tablespoon) to bring the mixture together to form a dough.

3 Divide the dough into eight pieces, using floured hands if necessary, and gently roll into small balls.

4 Pop on top of your soup, cover and simmer for 10 minutes.

5 Use a slotted spoon to carefully scoop the dumplings out. Divide the soup between the serving bowls, pop two dumplings onto each and enjoy!

Tip: Do remember to simmer and not boil the soup, otherwise the dumplings are likely to disintegrate.

Grissini Pastry Puffs

Makes: 8 *Vegetarian*
Preparation time: *10 minutes + 15 minutes baking*
Freezing: *recommended*

These are great nibbles to serve with soup. Choose the most appropriate variation to match the soup you are serving, or make a selection and everybody can choose their favourite!

FOR BASIC PASTRY PUFFS:
225 g (8 oz) puff pastry
1 beaten egg

FOR OLIVE AND SUN-DRIED TOMATO PUFFS:
12 pitted green olives
4 halves sun-dried tomatoes, finely chopped
¼ teaspoon dried oregano

FOR GRUYÈRE AND WALNUT PUFFS:
40 g (1½ oz) Gruyère cheese, grated
40 g (1½ oz) walnuts, chopped

FOR SESAME OR POPPY SEED PUFFS:
sesame or poppy seeds to sprinkle

1 Pre-heat the oven to Gas Mark 6/ 200°C/400°F. Lightly grease two baking trays.

2 On a lightly floured surface, roll out the pastry to measure 23 x 20 cm (9 x 8 inches). Cut into strips 23 x 2.5 cm (9 x 1 inches).

3 Place these on the baking trays, spaced apart. Brush with the beaten egg.

4 Scatter your chosen toppings over the strips and, using your fingers, press down lightly into the surface.

5 Bake in the centre of the oven for 15 minutes until puffy and golden. Cool slightly on a wire rack before serving warm, fresh from the oven.

Rarebit Croustades

Makes: 8 *Vegetarian*
Preparation time: *10 minutes + 10 minutes cooking*
Freezing: *not recommended*

Float these on top of soup as a garnish. Place the croustades in the serving bowl and pour the soup over the top (European style), or serve alongside as a side dish. These can be made while the soup is simmering and kept warm until you are ready.

FOR THE CROUSTADES:
8 x 2 cm- (¾ inch-) thick slices from day old
  French bread
olive oil for brushing

FOR THE RAREBIT:
1 tablespoon butter
1 tablespoon flour
3 tablespoons white wine or beer
½ teaspoon French mustard
80 g (3 oz) strong Cheddar cheese, grated
Worcestershire sauce
freshly ground black pepper

1 Pre-heat the grill to a medium setting.

2 Lightly brush one side of each piece of bread with oil. Place oiled sides up on the grill pan and grill until golden. Remove, turn each piece over and set to one side.

3 For the rarebit, melt the butter in a pan, add the flour and cook for 1 minute.

4 Gradually stir in the wine or beer to make a smooth sauce.

5 Add the mustard and, over a low heat, stir in a little of the cheese at a time, ensuring that it has melted before you add the next batch.

6 Remove from the heat as soon as all the cheese has been incorporated and season with a few drops of Worcestershire sauce and pepper.

7 Spread dessertspoonfuls of the rarebit mixture onto the untoasted side of the bread and return to the grill for about 4–5 minutes until golden, bubbling and irresistible!

Polenta, Pancetta and Sage Muffins

Makes: 10–12
Preparation time: *15 minutes + 20 minutes baking*
Freezing: *recommended*

Polenta gives these muffins a pleasantly 'gritty' texture and a beautiful yellow colour. There is no need to add any salt as the pancetta has plenty!

115 g (4 oz) polenta
115 g (4 oz) self-raising flour
2 teaspoons baking powder
½ teaspoon bicarbonate of soda
¼ teaspoon cayenne pepper
3 rashers pancetta, grilled until crisp
3 tablespoons chopped fresh sage
250 ml (8 fl oz) natural low fat yogurt
1 egg, beaten
80 g (3 oz) butter, melted
25 g (1 oz) grated Parmesan cheese

1 Pre-heat the oven to Gas Mark 6/ 200°C/400°F. Grease 12 muffin/individual Yorkshire pudding tins.

2 Place the polenta, flour, baking powder, bicarbonate and cayenne pepper in a bowl.

3 Crumble in the pancetta and add the chopped sage. Stir well.

4 Make a well in the centre and add the yogurt, egg, butter and most of the Parmesan. Taking a large metal spoon, quickly and carefully fold the ingredients together (over mixing will make the muffins tough).

5 Divide the mixture between the tins, filling each about two-thirds full. This will make 10–12 muffins, depending how large you like them. Sprinkle with the remaining Parmesan.

6 Bake in the centre of the oven for 15–20 minutes, until risen and golden. Turn out onto a wire rack and serve warm, fresh from the oven.

Illustrated on page 85.

Winter

Soups are part and parcel of winter time and often take centre stage, playing the main role in a meal and full of winter cheer. Their comforting aroma fills the kitchen with anticipation of a satisfying meal to come. They provide an internal warmth, their richness acting as a natural defence against the cold outside.

Puy Lentil and Bacon Soup

Serves: 4
Preparation time: *15 minutes + 40 minutes cooking*
Freezing: *recommended*

If you are limited for time use a can of green lentils instead and heat through with the stock and herbs for just 5 minutes. Ham can be substituted for the bacon.

1 tablespoon olive oil
3 rashers streaky bacon, snipped
1 onion, chopped
1 stick celery, chopped, including the leaves
115 g (4 oz) Puy lentils
1 tablespoon chopped fresh thyme
1 tablespoon chopped fresh parsley
850 ml (1½ pints) half strength ham or chicken
   stock (page 15)
salt
freshly ground black pepper

FOR THE GARNISH:
2 rashers crispy bacon, broken into pieces
1 hard boiled egg, chopped or grated
fresh parsley, chopped

1   Heat the oil in a large lidded saucepan, add the bacon, onion and celery and stir to coat. Cover and sweat for 10 minutes, shaking the pan occasionally.

2   Wash the lentils. Add to the pan with the thyme, parsley and stock. Bring to the boil, cover and simmer for 30 minutes.

3   Cool slightly before puréeing half the soup in a liquidiser.

4   Return the puréed soup to the pan. Mix together well and adjust seasoning. Heat through until piping hot.

5   Pour into warmed serving bowls and garnish with pieces of crispy bacon, chopped or grated hard boiled egg and a scattering of parsley.

Pork Goulash Soup

Serves: 4
Preparation time: *10 minutes + 45 minutes cooking*
Freezing: *recommended before adding cream*

This is a wonderfully warming soup. Serve with Dumplings (page 106), flavoured with caraway or fennel seeds, to make this into a meal.

1 tablespoon olive oil
1 Spanish onion, roughly chopped
1 red pepper, chopped into bite-sized chunks
225 g (8 oz) pork tenderloin
1 clove garlic, crushed
1 tablespoon flour
½ teaspoon smoked paprika
600 ml (1 pint) chicken stock (page 15)
400 g can chopped tomatoes
salt
freshly ground black pepper
4 tablespoons sour cream to serve

1 Heat the oil in a large lidded saucepan, add the onion and pepper and fry over a fairly high heat for about 10 minutes, until just beginning to brown.

2 Slice the pork into medallions and then cut these across so that you have thin strips. Add these to the pan and cook for a couple of minutes.

3 Stir in the garlic and cook for 1 minute.

4 Reduce the heat and stir in the flour. Cook for a further minute.

5 Add the paprika, stock and tomatoes, bring to the boil, cover and simmer for 30 minutes. If making dumplings, add these 10 minutes before the end of cooking.

6 Season to taste. Spoon into warmed serving bowls and place a tablespoonful of sour cream on each. Stir this through before starting to tuck in!

Creamy Chorizo and Sprout Soup

Serves: 4
Preparation time: *15 minutes + 30 minutes cooking time*
Freezing: *recommended before adding cream*

The chorizo dominates this recipe, so do adapt it to your personal preferences by adding perhaps just 50 g (2 oz) chorizo, and calling it Sprout and Chorizo Soup!

1 tablespoon olive oil
1 onion, chopped
80 g (3 oz) chorizo slices, quartered
850 ml (1½ pints) chicken stock (page 15)
450 g (1 lb) Brussel sprouts, bases scored
2 tablespoons single cream
salt
freshly ground black pepper
sprigs of parsley to garnish

1 Heat the oil in a large lidded saucepan. Fry the onion and chorizo in the oil for 8–10 minutes or until the onion is softened and the chorizo is crisp. Reserve a few pieces of chorizo for the garnish.

2 Stir in the stock and bring to the boil. Add the sprouts, cover and simmer for 20 minutes.

3 Allow to cool slightly before liquidising to a purée.

4 Stir in the cream and season to taste.

5 Return the soup to the rinsed out pan, re-heat gently until piping hot and pour into warmed serving bowls. Garnish with slices of reserved chorizo and sprigs of parsley.

Roasted Parsnip and Parmesan Soup

Serves: 4
Preparation time: *15 minutes + 45 minutes cooking*
Freezing: *recommended*

Parmesan gives this soup a 'rugged' texture. It also makes it incredibly rich and satisfying.

3 tablespoons olive oil
700 g (1½ lb) parsnips, cored and sliced into
   batons
1 medium onion, cut into wedges
40 g (1½ oz) Parmesan cheese, grated
2 rashers pancetta
850 ml (1½ pints) hot chicken stock (page 15)
salt
freshly ground black pepper
4 tablespoons double cream

1 Pre-heat the oven to Gas Mark 6/ 200°C/400°F. Pour the oil into a roasting tin and place on the top shelf of the oven for about 5 minutes until the oil is smokey hot.

2 Carefully tip the parsnips and onion into the tin, season and toss in the oil to coat. Roast for 30 minutes.

3 Sprinkle the Parmesan over the vegetables and stir it in. Lay the rashers of pancetta over the top. Cook for a further 10 minutes.

4 Remove the tin from the oven. Lift out the pancetta and set on one side for the garnish, along with a few crispy cheesy batons of parsnip.

5 In batches, pour the hot chicken stock into a liquidiser along with the parsnips and any juices or scrapings from the pan. Purée until smooth and season to taste.

6 Re-heat the soup gently, without boiling, until piping hot. Check seasoning and serve in warmed bowls topped with a spoonful of cream, half a slice of pancetta and the reserved cheesy parsnips.

The Number One Winter Soup

Serves: 6
Preparation time: *15 minutes + 55 minutes cooking.*
Freezing: *recommended*

This soup contains everything that you would expect in a winter soup – vegetables, bacon, lentils and chicken – a meal in itself!

1 tablespoon olive oil
1 tablespoon butter
4 rashers streaky bacon, snipped
1 boneless chicken thigh, diced
2 onions, chopped
2 cloves garlic, crushed
2 sticks celery, diced
2 carrots, diced
1 parsnip, diced
2 leeks, sliced
1.7 litres (3 pints) half strength chicken stock
   (page 15)
175 g (6 oz) red lentils, washed
2 tablespoons chopped fresh parsley
¼ teaspoon dried thyme
1 bay leaf
salt
freshly ground black pepper

1 Heat the oil and butter in a large lidded saucepan. Add the bacon and stir round until golden.

2 Add the chicken and cook for 3–4 minutes, turning, until browned.

3 Stir in the onions, garlic, celery, carrots, parsnip and leeks. Cover and sweat for 10 minutes.

4 Add the stock, lentils and herbs. Bring to the boil and cook, uncovered, for 10 minutes at a rolling boil. Reduce the heat, cover and carry on simmering for 30 minutes.

5 Adjust seasoning and ladle this luscious soup into warmed serving bowls.

Old Fashioned Barley, Ham and Vegetable Soup

Serves: 6
Preparation time: *15 minutes + 2 hours cooking*
Freezing: *not recommended*

A true soup that is left bubbling on the stove for a couple of hours, pervading the home with a comforting aroma of the promise of good food to come.

2 tablespoons olive oil
2 onions, chopped
2 leeks, sliced
2 medium carrots, diced
gammon shank (approximately 1 kg/2¼ lb)
150 g (5 oz) pearl barley
4 tablespoons chopped fresh parsley plus
    extra to garnish
½ teaspoon dried thyme
2 bay leaves
1.7 litres (3 pints) water
freshly ground black pepper
salt

1 Heat the oil in a large lidded saucepan, add the onions, leeks and carrots. Cover and sweat for 10 minutes, shaking the pan occasionally.

2 Add the gammon shank (complete with the rind unless there is an abundance of fat underneath it, in which case remove both), pearl barley, parsley, thyme, bay leaves and 1.2 litres (2 pints) of the water.

Season with pepper only at this stage. Bring to the boil, cover and simmer for 2 hours, stirring occasionally and topping up with the remaining water when necessary.

3 Remove the bay leaves and gammon shank. Allow the shank to cool slightly. Discard the skin, bones and any fat. Cut the ham into bite-sized pieces.

4 Stir the meat through the soup and re-heat. Check seasoning before ladling into warmed serving bowls and sprinkling with the extra parsley.

Tips: Gammon shank is very economical. To be on the safe side, soak overnight in case it is salty.

If you wish, lightly steam some cut French beans and stir them through the soup just before serving to give added colour and crunch.

Butterbean, Carrot and Rosemary Soup

Serves: a generous 4
Preparation time: *15 minutes + 40 minutes cooking.*
Freezing: *recommended*

This soup is beautifully subtle both in terms of colour and flavour. However, if you are a rosemary lover then you'll probably wish to increase the amount slightly.

2 tablespoons olive oil
1 onion, diced
1 clove garlic, sliced
350 g (12 oz) carrots, diced
2 sticks celery, sliced
700 ml (1¼ pints) chicken stock (page 15)
2 teaspoons chopped rosemary
1 bay leaf
410 g can butterbeans, rinsed and drained
salt
freshly ground black pepper
sprigs of rosemary to garnish

1 Heat the oil in a large lidded saucepan; add the onion, garlic, carrots and celery, cover and sweat for 10 minutes, shaking the pan occasionally.

2 Add the stock, rosemary and bay leaf, bring to the boil, cover, and simmer for 20 minutes.

3 Stir in the butterbeans and continue to simmer for a further 10 minutes.

4 Cool the soup slightly before puréeing in a liquidiser. Adjust seasoning to taste and serve garnished with a sprig of rosemary (complete with its pretty lavender-pink coloured flowers if possible).

Hot Pot Soup

Serves: 4
Preparation time: *15 minutes + 40 minutes cooking*
Freezing: *recommended*

A hearty soup that serves as a one-pot meal.

1 tablespoon oil
175 g (6 oz) lamb neck fillet, cut into chunks
1 onion, chopped
2 leeks, sliced
1 large carrot, diced
1 medium potato, diced
700 ml (1¼ pints) lamb stock (page 17)
1 tablespoon chopped fresh parsley
½ teaspoon dried thyme
1 bay leaf
salt
freshly ground black pepper
chopped fresh parsley to garnish

1 Heat the oil in a large lidded saucepan, add the lamb and fry for 2–3 minutes to brown. Remove from the pan with a slotted spoon and set aside.

2 Add a little more oil if necessary and sweat the onion, leeks, carrot and potato for 10 minutes.

3 Return the lamb to the pan with the stock and herbs. Bring the soup to the boil, cover and simmer for 30 minutes.

4 Check seasoning before serving in warmed bowls sprinkled with a little parsley.

Celery Soup with White Stilton and Apricots

Serves: 6
Preparation time: *15 minutes + 40 minutes cooking*
Freezing: *recommended*

A real winter soup, this has a wonderful flavour.

15 g (½ oz) butter
1 large onion, chopped
5 celery sticks, sliced
1 large potato
850 ml (1½ pints) chicken stock (page 15)
1 bay leaf
175 g (6 oz) white Stilton cheese with apricots
sugar to taste
salt
freshly ground black pepper

FOR THE GARNISH:
handful chopped celery leaves
15 g (½ oz) crumbled white Stilton cheese with
  apricots

1 Melt the butter in a large lidded saucepan, add the onion and celery, cover and sweat for 15 minutes, shaking the pan occasionally.

2 Add the potato, stock and bay leaf, bring to the boil and simmer for 20 minutes.

3 Over a low heat, blend in the Stilton and season with sugar, salt and pepper.

4 Cool slightly, then pour into a liquidiser and run until the soup is smooth and creamy.

5 Return to the rinsed out pan, re-heat and ladle into warmed serving bowls. Garnish with some celery leaves and crumbled cheese.

Jerusalem Artichoke Soup with Roasted Garlic

Serves: 4
Preparation time: *15 minutes + 50 minutes cooking*
Freezing: *recommended before adding cream*

Jerusalem artichokes are synonymous with soup, partly because of their ideal texture and partly because they are such a nuisance to peel that, scrubbed well, this is all the preparation needed.

1 head garlic
25 g (1 oz) butter
1 onion, chopped
450 g (1 lb) Jerusalem artichokes, scrubbed
   and chopped
850 ml (1½ pints) chicken stock (page 15)
150 ml (¼ pint) milk
4 tablespoons double cream, plus a little extra
   for garnishing
salt
freshly ground black pepper
fresh chives, snipped, to garnish

1 Pre-heat the oven to Gas Mark 5/ 170°C/320°F.

2 Break up the head of garlic into individual cloves and place them in a small roasting tin. Bake for 20 minutes until soft and golden.

3 Meanwhile, melt the butter in a large lidded saucepan; add the onion and sweat, covered, for 10 minutes.

4 Remove the garlic from the oven and, when cool enough to handle, use a sharp knife to slit the skins. Pop out the garlic purée inside. Add to the onion mixture with the artichokes, stock and milk. Bring to the boil, cover and simmer for 25 minutes.

5 Allow the soup to cool slightly before puréeing in a blender. Sieve and return to the rinsed out pan.

6 Stir in the cream and adjust seasoning to taste. Reheat gently and serve in warmed bowls garnished with snipped chives and an extra swirl of cream if you wish.

Blue Cheese Crumbles

Makes: approximately 36 biscuits *Vegetarian*
Preparation time: *15 minutes + 1 hour chilling + 15 minutes cooking*
Freezing: *freeze dough before baking*

These moreish biscuits are great nibbled with most soups.

175 g (6 oz) plain flour
1 teaspoon mustard powder
freshly ground black pepper
80 g (3 oz) softened butter
50 g (2 oz) St. Agur or similar creamy blue
cheese

1 Mix together the flour, mustard powder and pepper, and rub in the butter.

2 Cut the cheese into cubes, add to the bowl and rub in.

3 Bring the mixture together to form a dough, wrap in cling film and chill for about an hour.

4 Pre-heat the oven to Gas Mark 4/ 180°C/350°F.

5 Lightly flour the work surface and, using a rolling pin, roll the dough out into an oblong shape approximately 5 mm (¼ inch) thick. Cut into triangles or rectangular shapes to your chosen size. Using a slice, transfer to a greased baking sheet.

6 Cook in the centre of the oven for 12–15 minutes until golden. Transfer on to a wire rack to cool and crispen. Store in an airtight container for 2–3 days.

Sunflower Soda Bread

Makes: 1 x 900 g (2 lb) loaf *Vegetarian*
Preparation time: *10 minutes + 55–60 minutes cooking*
Freezing: *not recommended*

Made with the goodness of yogurt, sunflower seeds and honey, this loaf is quick to make as you do not have to wait for it to rise.

450 g (1 lb) malted brown flour
2 teaspoons bicarbonate of soda
½ teaspoon coarse sea salt
50 g (2 oz) butter
25 g (1 oz) toasted sunflower seeds
1 tablespoon clear honey
500 g pot natural yogurt
milk for brushing
untoasted sunflower seeds for sprinkling

1 Pre-heat the oven to Gas Mark 6/ 200°C/400°F. Grease a 900 g (2 lb) loaf tin.

2 Place the flour, bicarbonate of soda and salt in a large mixing bowl.

3 Rub in the butter until the mixture resembles fine breadcrumbs.

4 Stir in the sunflower seeds.

5 Make a well in the centre and add the honey and most of the yogurt. Mix to a soft dough, adding a little more yogurt if necessary. Tip out onto a floured work surface and lightly work into an oblong.

6 Place the dough in the prepared tin. Using a sharp knife, make a lengthways slit down the centre. Brush the loaf with milk and sprinkle generously with sunflower seeds.

7 Bake in the middle of the oven for 15 minutes, then reduce the oven temperature to Gas Mark 4/180°C/350°F and cook for a further 40–45 minutes.

8 Cool on a wire rack and serve sliced with butter. This bread is best eaten on the day that it is made.

Tip: For a change, substitute the sunflower seeds with pumpkin seeds or pine nuts. Roasting them first gives a much better flavour.

Illustrated on page 117.

Tortilla Strips

Serves: as many as you like! *Vegetarian*
Preparation time: *5 minutes + 5 minutes cooking*
Freezing: *not recommended*

These are very easy to make — alter the design of the topping to complement the soup that you intend to serve them with.

flour tortillas
melted butter
topping such as black onion seeds, sesame
  seeds or clear honey and Cajun spice

1 Pre-heat the oven to Gas Mark 4/
  180°C/350°F.

2 Brush the tortillas with the melted butter.

3 Sprinkle the tortillas with the topping of your
  choice. If using seeds, press down lightly so
  that they don't fall off. For the honey, brush
  tortillas lightly and then sprinkle the spice over
  sparingly.

4 On a board, use a sharp knife to slice the
  tortillas into 3 cm (1¼ inch) wide strips.

5 Place the strips on a baking tray and bake
  in the centre of the oven for 4–5 minutes
  – watch them carefully to ensure they don't
  burn.

6 Transfer to a wire rack to cool, they will
  crispen as they do so. They can be stored in
  an airtight container for 2–3 days.

Naan Bread with Fennel and Black Onion Seeds

Makes: 8 *Vegetarian*
Preparation time: *30 minutes + 1 hour proving + 20–30 minutes cooking in batches*
Freeing: *recommended*

These beautifully fragrant 'slippers' would be delicious with any number of soups. Unlike traditional bread they only require one proving.

50 g (2 oz) butter
1 small fennel bulb, finely diced
450 g (1 lb) strong white bread flour
1 sachet easy blend yeast
1 teaspoon baking powder
2 teaspoons sugar
½ teaspoon coarse sea salt
1 teaspoon black onion seeds
1 egg, beaten
4 tablespoons natural yogurt
200 ml (7 fl oz) hand-hot milk plus a little for brushing

1 Melt the butter in a pan, add the fennel, cover and sweat for 10 minutes until softened, shaking the pan occasionally. Allow to cool until tepid or cold but with the butter still melted.

2 Combine the flour, yeast, baking powder, sugar, salt and onion seeds in a large bowl.

3 Make a well in the centre of the flour mixture and add the fennel and butter, egg, yogurt and milk. Mix together to form a soft dough.

4 Turn out onto a floured work surface and knead until smooth, about 10 minutes. Place in an oiled polythene bag and leave in a warm place for about 1 hour to prove, until doubled in size.

5 Heat the oven to Gas Mark 7/220°C/425°F. Grease 2–3 baking trays.

6 Divide the dough into eight pieces. Using floured hands, fashion each into a teardrop shape measuring about 20 cm (8 inches) long. Mould so that the middle is thinner than the edge to achieve the classic naan appearance.

7 Place the breads on baking trays, spaced well apart, and brush with milk. Bake in batches, in the middle of the oven, for 10 minutes each. Cover those not being cooked at the time. The naan should be puffy and golden. Cool slightly on a wire rack and serve warm.

Tip: The fennel makes the dough soft, but a little wet, so use plenty of extra flour on your work surface for kneading.

Illustrated on page 121.

Potato and Rosemary Bread

Serves: 8–10 *Vegetarian/Vegan*
Preparation time: *15 minutes + 90–100 minutes proving + 30 minutes baking*
Freezing: *recommended*

Potato gives this bread a beautifully smooth crust and soft texture rather than actually flavouring it. It partners vegetable soups particularly well.

175 g (6 oz) cold cooked potatoes, mashed
450 g (1 lb) strong white bread flour
1 sachet easy blend yeast
1 teaspoon coarse sea salt, plus extra for sprinkling
1½ tablespoons chopped rosemary
300 ml (½ pint) warm water
2 tablespoons olive oil, plus extra for brushing

1 Mix together the mashed potato, flour, yeast, salt and rosemary in a large bowl.

2 Add the water and oil and mix to a soft dough. Turn out onto a floured surface and knead for about 10 minutes to give a smooth dough. The potato tends to make this dough a little sticky, so you will probably need to add more flour every now and then.

3 Place the dough in an oiled polythene bag, with plenty of room for it to expand. Leave in a warm place for about an hour until doubled in size.

4 Knock back the dough to expel the air and shape it into a round. Place on a greased baking sheet. Slash a cross shape on the top, brush with olive oil and sprinkle with a little salt. Cover again and prove for 30–40 minutes until well risen.

5 Pre-heat the oven to Gas Mark 7/ 220°C/425°F.

6 Bake the loaf for 10 minutes in the centre of the oven. Reduce the oven temperature to Gas Mark 5/190°C/375°F and cook for a further 20 minutes until golden.

7 Cool on a wire rack. Cut the loaf into wedges and serve whilst still warm.

Tip: Floury potatoes, such as King Edward or Maris Piper, work well in this recipe.

Caramelised Onion and Cheese Bread

Serves: 8 *Vegetarian*
Preparation time: *30 minutes + 1¾ hours proving + 25 minutes cooking*
Freezing: *recommended*

This bread, in the shape of a ring, makes an inviting centrepiece to the table and is an excellent accompaniment to many of the soups in this book.

350 g (12 oz) strong white bread flour
1 sachet easy blend yeast
1 teaspoon sugar
½ teaspoon coarse sea salt
25 g (1 oz) butter
1 egg, beaten
150 ml (¼ pint) milk, plus extra for brushing
poppy seeds

FOR THE FILLING:
25 g (1 oz) butter
2 onions, halved and thinly sliced
150 g (5 oz) Emmental cheese, grated
freshly ground black pepper

1 Place the flour, yeast, sugar and salt in a large bowl. Rub in the butter. Make a well in the centre and add the egg and milk. Mix to a soft dough.

2 Turn the dough out onto a work surface and knead for about 10 minutes until smooth. Place in an oiled polythene bag and leave in a warm place to prove until doubled in size, about 1 hour.

3 Meanwhile, make the filling. Melt the butter in a pan, add the onions and fry for roughly 20 minutes over a medium heat, until the onions are a deep golden brown. Set aside to cool.

4 Lightly grease a baking tray – make sure that it has a continuous lip (when the cheese melts during cooking it releases a lot of excess fat that could drip onto the oven floor).

5 On a lightly floured surface, roll out the dough into an oblong 38 x 23 cm (15 x 9 inches). Do not knock the dough back first as this makes it more difficult to work with.

6 Scatter the onions over the dough, spreading them almost to the edges. Sprinkle the cheese over the cooled onions and grind over some black pepper. Roll the dough up tightly, starting from a long edge, and form into a circle, tucking the ends in and moistening them with a little milk to help them stick.

7 Transfer the ring to the baking tray. Make cuts from the outside towards the centre at 5 cm (2 inch) intervals, penetrating nearly three-quarters of the way through (scissors are good for this). You should have eight sections. Take hold of one section at a time and twist it sideways so that the filling is facing slightly upwards. Repeat with the other sections to form a wheel-like effect.

8 Cover and prove for about 45 minutes, until doubled in size.

9 Pre-heat the oven to Gas Mark 6/ 200°C/400°F.

10 Brush the bread ring with a little milk and sprinkle with the poppy seeds. Bake in the middle of the oven for 25 minutes until golden.

11 Cool slightly on a wire rack and serve warm.

Index